D1065185

Marriage is for Loving

Addison-Wesley Publishing Company
Reading, Massachusetts • Menlo Park, California
London • Amsterdam • Don Mills, Ontario • Sydney

Muriel James

Marriage is for Loving

Library of Congress Cataloging in Publication Data

James, Muriel.
Marriage is for loving.

Includes index.
1. Marriage. I. Title.
HQ734.J34 301.42 78-73118
ISBN 0-201-03454-9
ISBN 0-201-03455-7 pbk.

ISBN 0-201-03454-9 H
ISBN 0-201-03455-7 P
ABCDEFGHIJ-DO-79

All of life is for loving
not just marriage
So I thank all who have loved me
from their hearts
And I send you love from mine.

Muriel James
Lafayette, California

Part One MARRIAGE AND THE PAST

Contents

Part One

We were very tired, we were very merry—
We had gone back and forth all night on the ferry;
And you ate an apple, and I ate a pear,
From a dozen of each we had bought somewhere;
And the sky went wan, and the wind came cold,
And the sun rose dripping, a bucketful of gold.[1]

Edna St. Vincent Millay

Chapter I

"Do you love me?"
"Of course I love you!"
"Well, you sure don't say it often."
"What do you want me to do? Say it every day?"
"Yes, I think I do."
"That's silly."
"Maybe so, but I really feel that way."
"OK, OK."
"Maybe you don't even want to be married anymore."
"Of course I do. You know I do. Now you're being ridiculous."

Marriage is for Loving—Or is it?

And so it goes. The constant need people have for reassurance, that they are loved and that marriage is important. Many want to believe that marriage is for loving. After all, falling in love is an exciting, wonderful, magical experience. Songwriters from Cole Porter ("That Old Black Magic Called Love") to the Beatles ("All You Need Is Love") have recognized and profited from our fascination with love's magical qualities.

For many, love *is* magic, and marriage is the natural "happy ending" to falling in love. Yet falling in love and staying in love are two quite separate processes. When people face problems in their marriages, the magic may quickly vanish and difficult questions begin to surface:

Who are we and how did we get this way? Why do we sometimes feel trapped? What do we need to be *free from* so that we will be *free to* become the persons we want to be? Where did we get our views of marriage anyway?

What are we doing here and now? What's going on with us? How do we find the courage to recognize our needs and how might these needs be fulfilled? How do we identify our problems and look for solutions? What do we need to do to get closer to each other?

Where are we going in the future? Is there hope for us? What is hope all about? How do we find hope when we're feeling hopeless? What does it all mean?

Freedom from the past, courage to face the present, hope for the future—understanding all three is important in building a strong, loving marriage. Therefore, I have organized this book to help you closely examine the past in light of freedom, the present in light of courage, and the future in light of hope.

Many people live in their past; I know I have from time to time. I've also lived in the future, daydreaming of how my life might change. But both the past and future can be incorporated into the present, making it a better, more loving place to be.

Marriage is an age-old institution that is facing new times. With the divorce rate skyrocketing and more people choosing to live together without marriage, many wonder whether marriage will survive. I think that it will, and I have written this book to support those people who are working to make their marriages successful, loving ones. The process is often difficult, sometimes overwhelming, and it demands courage. I certainly don't have all of the answers, but I do have some insights that make sense to me and that I want to share with you.

Some of the examples come from my own marital experiences and from those of my friends. Even more of my insights and examples come from the many students and trainees I have had in classes and from the many individuals and couples that have come to me for counseling. (Naturally, these examples are disguised.) For twenty years, as a California-licensed marriage, family, and child counselor, I have listened, learned, taught, and shared. I am deeply grateful to those who have entrusted me with their dreams, their hopes, their fears, their struggles, their failures and successes, their courage and commitment.

A number of people, including my editor, suggested that, because my life is interesting to many, I include some personal examples. Whether or not to do this has been a hard decision. I was brought up not to talk about personal matters and, to me, marriage is very personal. But loving requires openness and honesty, and I've decided I can be more open with who I am, where I've been, and where I might be going—in my life and in my marriage.

I remember being young and imagining marriage to be the most exciting thing in the world. I was one of those children who thought that people got married and lived happily ever after. It wasn't what I observed; it was what I daydreamed about.

My parents acted as if they were close and loving friends. Most of the time conflict was minimal. They enjoyed music and books together, camping together, friends together, and their three children.

But then my father became infatuated with someone else, and the world seemed to fall apart for the rest of the family. Little was said about the divorce, although emotional agony permeated our house in San Francisco. It wasn't easy; it hurt. But we survived.

After the divorce, my father married the other woman. Within a few years the romance faded and their marriage began to disintegrate. At night, Father started to drive around the block where we lived. Mother lighted candles in the window to signify that he was welcome. Yet he didn't come back. Too much pride, I suppose. Arguments with his second wife and his sudden death have remained a mystery to me, a tragedy that I think might have been averted.

Since that time I have thought intensely about marriage. Although my childhood experiences are past, they sometimes still strongly influence me. When I am aware of the influences, I am free to choose how to respond. When I am not aware, I am, in a sense, a prisoner of my past.

I've been married three times. The first time, I was seventeen. I had graduated from high school at sixteen and didn't know what to do with myself. I was intensely shy and withdrawn, fearful of almost everything and everybody. Then I happened to meet someone who was ten years older. He said all the things to me that I wanted to hear, and I was infatuated. Marriage seemed a convenient answer to the question of how to spend the rest of my life. We were married secretly; I didn't dare tell my parents until six months later, when we were married again publicly.

At nineteen I had my first child, four years later my second, and then the world fell apart again. I lost my husband and my father in a short time. Neither one left money, insurance, or any other kind of financial security. Suddenly I had myself, two children, and my mother to support. There was no one to turn to. I had no skills. I didn't know about social agencies; if I had, pride probably would have kept me from using them.

For the next year, four of us lived in a garret, then in a tiny apartment. Someone was always sick and we were usually hungry. We got our clothes from secondhand stores. Often I worked two eight-hour jobs so that we could afford to eat a bit better. At last we were able to rent a house. Slowly we made it through, with the will to live and the grace of God.

It was then that I met the man who was to become my second husband and the father of my third child. There were a lot of good times in that marriage and some painful ones, too. After eighteen years we were divorced and I lived as a single parent again for the next four years.

During my second marriage, when I was about thirty-three, I decided to get a formal education, and I soon became competent in several fields. I have always worked in addition to keeping house and being wife and mother. Sometimes the jobs— such as teacher or safety engineer—called for me to be outside the home; sometimes they were jobs I could handle from the house, such as organizing a direct-mail advertising company. Despite these new-found competencies, however, I still felt very shy, inadequate, and often fearful.

Then, in 1958, I was introduced to Eric Berne, originator of the psychological theory and method called Transactional Analysis. My life began to change quickly. At last I had a tool to use to analyze myself and other people in any situation. I began to feel more confidence in myself and my own decisions. A great sense of personal freedom came with this new knowledge and helped me discover new sources of courage and vitality within me.

Although I had thought I never wanted to be married again, I met someone who had four almost-grown children and who had been divorced for several years. I decided to risk loving again. And in 1965 I married for the third time. I'm still married, and I expect to stay married until one of us dies. Problems? Of course. No life is without them. Solutions? Naturally! And I'm continually discovering new ones. Love? For sure! Because I've found that marriage is for loving, and that's what this book is all about—loving and other options.

Speaking of options, I clearly remember the Thanksgiving Day that my daughter-in-law phoned me long distance. Angry and tearful, she expressed her fear that her marriage was collapsing. She and her husband were exhausted and ill after moving with their new baby to a city distant from friends and family. For several days they had been living without lights and heat during a storm, and, with the restoration of power on Thanksgiving Day, she had tackled the job of cooking her first turkey dinner. When she proudly presented the fruits of her labor, her husband unthinkingly criticized the gravy for not being "the kind Mom used to make." Naturally, it was the kind *her* Mom used to make.

The tension of this situation could have escalated into a battle if we hadn't recognized that the current problem was related to the past and that the future situation *could* be free of that kind of unhappiness. So we talked about gravy options: two kinds of gravy, alternating the two kinds on different occasions, choosing one gravy that everyone found acceptable, finding a new recipe, or, as a last resort, giving up gravy entirely!

We're now able to laugh with feelings of tenderness toward each other when we recall that day. How simple it suddenly became to change our perspective and rediscover a sense of hope when we discussed the five gravy choices that would be possible in the future.

Gravy may never be an issue in your marriage. It might be money, children, sex, clothes, or the car—or who takes out the garbage, or wipes up after the dog, or locks the door at night, or repairs the leaky faucet. Whatever the problems are, and however they get solved or not solved, they usually relate to the past of your marriage and, if left to simmer, will affect its future.

The past, present, and future of your marriage

The first part of this book focuses on your personal past and the cultural past of marriage in general. This will help you become aware of how the past influences your current views on marriage. Being in touch with that past can free you from its constraints. The past of any marriage includes childhood experiences and expectations, a courtship, the marriage ceremony itself, the first night, and the early years, but it also contains the historical events and laws that have shaped our contemporary views of marriage.

In the second part of this book, you can examine the *present* of your marriage—the needs most people have, the problems they face, and the intimacy they must develop to solve those problems. A here-and-now marriage is constantly becoming stronger as the partners strive to understand their needs and seek solutions as difficulties arise. A here-and-now marriage is dynamic, active, and courageous. It is learning how to love in the present, no matter what.

What about the possible *future* of your marriage? Part Three shows you how to turn dreams into reality and how to plan for excitement, warmth, tenderness, and caring, in the future as well as now. With hope, you can release more of your will to live and the courage to live your marriage more fully.

Each of the three parts of the book concludes with a chapter that offers many new ideas and exercises to help you gain insight into your marriage. These "do-it-yourself-marriage-counselor" chapters are intended to give you techniques to make your marriage more satisfying. Some, but not all, of the theory and exercises use Transactional Analysis, but in different ways from my other books.

It would be great if you would read this book with your partner, your partner-to-be, or even your has-been partner (if you have a friendly relationship). And it would be fine to read it alone. Whether you're thinking about marriage or not, you are likely to discover useful insights into yourself as an individual, as a partner, or as a potential partner.

Marriage and loving are important to me. I hope they are also important to you and that we both live up to this affirmation. I want this for us because I believe that *how* we live a marriage is a mirror that reflects the depths of how we love.

Chapter 2

"I'm going to the store to choose paint for the kitchen."

"Oh no you're not! I am!"

"What do you mean?"

"A man's home is his castle. That's what I mean."

"Since when and so what?"

"Since always. So I'll decide on the color."

"I don't think that's fair."

"That's the way it's always been."

"So why keep it that way?"

"It was good enough for my grandparents, so it's good enough for me."

"Oh, honey! You sound so old fashioned."

"Well, maybe I am."

The Roots of Marriage

Currently, there is a renaissance in the study of marriage, a renewed interest in an age-old institution that has evolved from a union designed principally for convenience to one based on loving and sharing. Every marriage today is rooted in religious, ethnic, racial, cultural, and family pasts. Our points of view, our traditions, our life-styles, our child-rearing practices, and our sexual roles all have their roots in history. To understand the present, it's interesting, even fascinating, to look at how marriage has changed through the ages, and that's what this chapter does. It briefly describes cultural similarities and differences that have affected the views we have today.

Marriage in ancient times

Marriage for love is a relatively modern idea. In ancient cultures marriage was principally for convenience. During the prehistoric period, before the emergence of agricultural societies, men and women hunted together in small bands or as family units, and it was convenient for some to hunt and for some to remain behind to cook and tend the fire. All of the earliest humans were hunters and gatherers; today, a few societies (the Australian Aborigines and the Bushmen of the Kalahari Desert in Africa) still are.

Around 8000 B.C. there was a major and widespread cultural change that radically affected people's views of marriage. From hunting and gathering, where children were often a burden, the people switched to cultivating crops, domesticating animals, and forming agricultural settlements. Here children were needed: as on today's farms, they could tend animals, draw water, and hoe crops. Ownership of property then became important and laws of inheritance developed rapidly.

Urban civilization and the ability to read and write led to the first recorded marriage laws, which were in the Code of Hammurabi, a code of civil and criminal laws developed in ancient Babylonia around 4000 B.C. The code shows that marriage was both an economic transaction—women belonged to their fathers until they were sold to husbands—and a contract between husband and wife. Women who were barren were allowed to choose female servants to bear children, whom the wives then claimed as their own. Husbands, in turn, were permitted to take concubines if their wives refused this arrangement.

As in all ancient cultures, arranged marriages and dowries were common. The groom paid a price, often a parcel of land, which was given back to the couple for a nest egg. If the husband wished a divorce, however, both the dowry and any children became the property of the wife. Court action was also possible.

A husband could accuse his spouse of being a bad wife and thus make her a slave. In turn, she could accuse him of cruelty. If the dispute could not be settled, the Babylonians had a simple solution—the ordeal of water. If the accused could float, then he or she was obviously protected by the gods and thus innocent. The reverse was accepted as equally conclusive proof of guilt.

In ancient Egypt, too, marriage was frequently a matter of economic and political expediency. Brothers and sisters often married to keep real estate or an inherited official government position in the family. It was a matriarchal

culture; inheritance was always passed through the female line, and marriage agreements often gave brides the property belonging to the grooms. Many Pharaohs married their sisters or daughters to obtain the throne and to protect the blood line and inheritance. This custom continued through the Roman conquest of Egypt in 30 B.C. For example, Cleopatra (69–30 B.C.) married first her older brother and then, after his death, her younger brother. These marriages entitled each, in turn, to rule Egypt. When Julius Caesar married her, he had the same privileges, as did Mark Antony, who was her last husband.

Egyptian marriage was not exclusively a businesslike transaction. The poetry and love songs of ancient Egypt reveal a strong inclination toward romanticism and love. Different in style from our love songs of today ("If I kiss her and her mouth is open, I am happy even without beer."), the meaning is much the same.

In many of these songs, the words "brother" and "sister" are used and often carry the meaning "beloved":

> *I see my sister coming and my heart rejoices,*
> *My arms are opened wide to embrace her*
> *and my heart rejoices upon its place . . .*
> *When the mistress comes to me*
> *If I embrace her and her arms are opened*
> *It is for me as if I were one that is from Punt [land of perfums] . . .*[1]

Sanctified Hebrew marriage

The Hebrew people were closely related to Babylon and Egypt. Nomads from the Mesopotamian valley, they migrated around 1800 B.C. to Canaan, currently known as Israel.

For the ancient Hebrew people, too, romance and marriage were often poignantly linked. The Old Testament recounts numerous stories of courtships and marriages—those that succeeded as well as those that failed. In The Song of Solomon, the dialogue of the bride and groom at their wedding is romantic and passionate. "O that you would kiss me with the kisses of your mouth!" the bride says, "For your love is better than wine." The groom replies, "Behold, you are beautiful my love. . . . Your eyes are doves behind your veil. . . . Your lips are like a scarlet thread, your breasts are like two fawns, twins of a gazelle that feed among the lilies. . . . You have ravished my heart, my sister, my bride." (Song of Sol. 4 : 1–7)

The story of Jacob and Rachel is perhaps one of the most touching biblical love stories. Jacob, grandson of Abraham, lived with his parents in the land of Canaan. When it was time for him to marry, his mother sent him to her homeland in northern Mesopotamia to seek a wife from among her own people. There he met and fell in love with Rachel. According to custom, he had to work seven years for her father to get permission to marry his beloved. However, on the wedding night, a cruel deception took place: Rachel's father tricked Jacob into marrying her older, less attractive sister. Still in love with Rachel, Jacob worked another seven years so at last he could marry her. According to the story, the years of service "seemed unto him but a few days, for the love he had to her." (Gen. 29 : 20)

While romance played a part in marriages in early Hebrew times, family and financial considerations were certainly not overlooked. Cousins often married to keep livestock and property in the family. Chastity was expected, incestuous relations were forbidden, and impotency was grounds for divorce. Widows were pitied; thus, the levirate laws, which required a brother of the deceased or next of kin to marry a widow, were established. If the man refused, a woman could, in the presence of a council of elders, remove his shoe and spit in his face.

The Hebrews' view of marriage may be characterized as more integrated and all-encompassing than that of other early peoples. It was neither a civil nor a religious contract. Marriage was a joyous event—the prelude to sexual enjoyment, procreation, family love, and happiness. It was a sanctification (*kiddushim*) based on lofty ideals. The Hebrews' belief in one God, Yahweh, and in their status as His chosen people was reflected in their views of marriage; the words about marriage were often used as a symbol of this relationship.

However, all was not milk and honey in ancient Israel. Although women were protected, cared for, and respected, they were also held in contempt for their sexuality, which was considered a defilement. As early as 600–400 B.C., the writer of the biblical book of Job lamented: "Man that is born of a woman is of few days, and full of trouble. . . . Who can bring a clean thing out of an unclean? . . . How then can a man be righteous before God? How can he who is born of woman be clean?" (Job 14:1, 4; 25:4)

This ancient Jewish tradition, strongly masculine and anti-feminist, is still influential today. The daily prayer still recited by orthodox Jewish men is: "Barush Atah Adonai, Elohaynu Melek Ha-Olam, Sheloh Assani Yishah." (Blessed art Thou, O Lord, Our God and King of the Universe, that Thou didst not create me a woman.)

Open and restrictive marriages in Greece

The Greek and Hebrew peoples were historical counterparts, yet they viewed marriage in quite different ways. Greek civilization was divided essentially between its two major centers, Athens and Sparta, two city-states that differed radically in government, in the established rights and duties of citizens, and in marriage laws and attitudes. Whereas Spartan marriages were "open" even by modern standards, Athenian marriages were extremely restrictive.

Spartan men and women participated in a unique marriage ritual that began with the staged abduction of the bride to her new home. The groom, however, continued to live in the soldiers' barracks until age thirty, sneaking out only after dark to join his wife. Even more surprising, he ate in the mess hall until age sixty. The rationale behind this unique custom was to conserve the soldiers' strength, thought to be sapped by excessive intercourse. If a couple did not have children, another man would be invited in to impregnate the wife. If a married man did not want to sleep with his wife, but did want to have children by someone else, this was acceptable if permission was granted.

Since Spartan men were first and foremost soldiers and therefore often off to war, upper-class women gained much political power and sexual freedom. Some women had two households and two husbands and thus became owners of extensive tracts of land. Although monogamy was the generally accepted norm at this time, marriage was largely open and the sharing of husbands and wives with friends was neither unusual nor condemned.

Athenian women lived far more restrictive lives than did their counterparts in Sparta. Whereas Spartan women had minimal household responsibilities and hence a large degree of freedom, women in Athens were kept as objects, financially and legally dependent on fathers and husbands for reasons of family economics. Their role was to provide children and to keep the family line pure. Thus, for many centuries husbands had the right to kill their wives if they were adulterous. Women, and hence marriage, were generally downgraded. In an observation indicative of the prevailing view, Pythagoras, in the sixth century B.C., noted: "There is a good principle, which has created order, light, and man; and a bad principle, which has created chaos, darkness, and woman."[2]

Although Homer treated love in marriage favorably in the *Iliad* and *Odyssey,* other Greek writers were far less charitable. Love in marriage is sometimes ridiculed. Palladas, a poet, (368–431 B.C.) wrote: "Marriage brings a man only two happy days. The day he takes his bride to bed and the day he lays her in her grave."[3]

Power and law in Roman marriage

Romulus, the legendary founder of Rome, is credited with the first Roman marriage laws. Dionysius of Halicarnassus, writing in 25 B.C., described these laws and the power they gave to the husband:

> *The law was to this effect, that a woman joined to her husband by a holy marriage should share in all his possessions and sacred rites. . . . This law obliged both the married women, as having no other refuge, to conform themselves entirely to the temper of their husbands and the husbands to rule their wives as necessary and inseparable possessions.*[4]

For most of Roman history, husbands had full power over their wives, an extension of the power Roman fathers exerted over their female children. A wife's status was that of *imbecillitas,* from which the word imbecile comes. Power in Rome was the law, and that law regarded marriage as exclusively for procreation and for the purpose of keeping inherited property in the family. Roman law was to become the basis for English common law many centuries later, and though the severity of punishment would diminish, the rights of husbands remained comprehensive.

As in Athens, a Roman husband had the right to kill a wife who failed in her marital duties or disobeyed the strict rules governing a woman's conduct. (Divorce was nonexistent until 231 B.C.) The ancient laws granted this right if a wife committed adultery, drank an abortifacient to rid herself of an unborn child, or counterfeited the keys to her husband's wine cellar. Roman women were strictly forbidden to drink wine, as "any woman who drinks wine immoderately closes her heart to every virtue and opens it to every vice."[5]

Writing in A.D. 9, historian Dio Cassius neatly summed up the Roman attitude toward marriage and the role a woman was intended to play. His statements reflect beliefs that prevailed for centuries and, in part, sound curiously similar to the traditional vows used in many wedding ceremonies today:

> *For is there anything better than a wife who is chaste, domestic, a good housekeeper, a rearer of children; one to gladden you in health, to tend you in sickness; to be your partner in good fortune, to console you in misfortune; to restrain the mad passion of youth, and to temper the unreasonable harshness of old age?*[6]

Conflicting attitudes in the early Christian era

Attitudes regarding marriage in the early Christian era, unlike those of Old Testament times, were seldom linked to romance and love. In fact, most early Christians seemed to have taken a rather dim view of marriage.

In the early Christian era there were three popular beliefs on marriage. The first was that it is God's gift, and propagation its purpose. Today many people still believe this. Others distort the argument. They may declare it to be a "sacred duty" to have large families when increased population is only wanted for industrial or military purposes.

The second common belief was that marriage is a necessary evil, "better to marry than to burn," ("burn" meaning to be consumed by passion.) "Gratification of passion" was based on the realistic awareness that physical intercourse was a basic need, desired by a large portion of any population, that therefore needed to be sanctioned in some way. Many marriages today, especially of adolescents, are based on this same belief.

The third belief about marriage was that it should be totally avoided. This belief became common because so many early Christians truly expected an imminent "second coming" of Christ. They thought they needed to be free of marriage responsibilities so that they could dedicate themselves to a religious life. Today marriage is often avoided for the same reason or because it might interfere with career advancement or some other interest.

Many marriage laws were changed radically. Polygamy and levirate marriages, for example, were no longer tolerated. The polygamy of the Old Testament patriarchs had been justified as a cultural necessity, a means of populating the world with "the chosen people." Tertullian (A.D. 160–230), an influential writer, cleverly argued that if God had intended polygamous relationships to exist, he would not have stopped with one rib from Adam to create Eve; he would have used several ribs and provided Adam with several wives.

By the second century, criticism of marriage had intensified. It was now branded "the work of Satan," with woman's body the focus of evil. Tertullian claimed that woman was a temple built over a sewer:

> *Woman, you are the devil's doorway. You have led astray one whom the devil would not dare attack directly. It is your fault that the Son of God had to die; you should always go in mourning and in rags."*[7]

The rise of monasticism in about A.D. 370 did nothing to improve religious notions of marriage. Clerics, who wielded great influence, were opposed to sexual pleasure as well as marriage. Even married couples were encouraged to renounce intercourse in favor of a life of celibacy and chastity, an attitude that continued throughout the Middle Ages.

Darkness in the Middle Ages

The invasion of the Roman Empire by northern barbarian tribes began in A.D. 376. (The word *barbarian* was used in a derogatory sense by Romans to describe anyone outside of Greek and Roman culture.) Throughout the fourth and fifth centuries, these pagan tribes overran the Roman Empire; consequently, each introduced its own particular marriage customs and conceptions.

In the Germanic tradition, for example, marriage was monogamous and adultery by either husband or wife was considered a punishable offense. The Franks, on the other hand, approved of polygamy and allowed brides to be bought and sold. It was, however, almost universally assumed that marriage in general was for family, economic, and sexual convenience.

By the late fifth century, the western Roman Empire had collapsed and the period now referred to as the Middle Ages had begun. The transition from tribal to national identities would take centuries. As royal power increased, the feudal tribal lord lost some of his absolute authority, including the right to decide about the marriages of his serfs. Marriages of companionship became possible, especially in the lower classes. Although the church still maintained its position that women, as descendents of Eve, were evil, a liberalizing tendency was under way.

By the late Middle Ages, a new romantic spirit was emerging. "Courtly" or "knightly" love, a movement that seems to have been first popularized by the troubadours of southern France, spread through the royal courts of England, France, and Germany. The code of courtly love was highly conventionalized: chaste, beautiful, and generally unattainable noblewomen were adored and suffered for by equally noble, gallant, and courageous knights. The principles of courtly love were embodied in such medieval romances as the allegorical "Romance of the Rose" and the true-life story of French theologian Pierre Abelard and his lover Heloise.

Abelard and Heloise married against the rule of the church and suffered terribly for their act. Abelard was castrated and became a monk; Heloise isolated herself in a convent. Still, they continued to correspond, and their famous exchange of love letters fueled the fires of courtly love further. Spurred on by such stories, knights and courtiers idealized and romanticized both warfare and women, often intermingling the two by viewing their noble deeds as performed for "the sake" of a lady. They were committed to loyalty, chivalry, bravery, justice, and continence; they believed in protecting the oppressed, fighting for their noblewomen (who were usually married and thus unattainable), and advancing Christianity, especially against the Muslims.

At the same time, many scholars were rejecting romanticism. For example, Sir Thomas Aquinas (1225–1274), an Italian philosopher and theologian whose writings have been very influential since the late Middle Ages, adapted the earlier philosophy of Aristotle that viewed women as misbegotten males, "defective and accidental . . . a male gone awry." Accordingly, he believed that children should be taught to respect their fathers more than their mothers. Wives, for their part, were admonished to keep their "husband's person . . . in clean linen," and a wife was one who "warms him by a good fire, washes his feet, fetches fresh shoes and stockings for him, good food and drink, gives him plenty of attentions, a comfortable bed, white sheets, a nightcap, fur covers, and the cheer of other delights, privy frolics, lovings, and secret matters which I shan't mention."[8]

Emerging freedom in the Renaissance and Reformation

Social mobility was severely restricted in the Middle Ages; people were born into a particular class and had little or no chance to improve their station. Not until the cultural and intellectual movement known as the Renaissance did individuals begin to experience the possibilities of new personal freedoms in all spheres of their lives. The emphasis of the Renaissance, which began in about A.D. 1400 and lasted for two hundred years, was a new humanism. People began to think in new ways, and what they were thinking was often contrary to what the political and ecclesiastical authorities held as true.

Although marriage during the Renaissance remained a primarily financial arrangement, new sexual and spiritual overtones emerged. The sexual emphasis identified women with Eve; the spiritual emphasis with the Virgin Mary.

Upper-class women enjoyed new freedoms. Gradually they began to dress erotically, use cosmetics without fear or guilt, and attend universities. Printed books became increasingly available and both lay men and women, not just the clergy, were encouraged to educate themselves. New freedoms spawned new thoughts: people viewed themselves as individuals with certain rights.

There was a darker side of the coin for women at this time, however. While some women were elevated and given more freedom, others began to be hunted out as witches, accused of being like "sinful Eve" and full of "lust." Witch hunting, sometimes a ploy used by husbands to rid themselves of unwanted wives, started in the Alps in the fifteenth century, where women preachers of the Waldensian group dared to establish their own religious rituals. They were persecuted by two Dominican inquisitors, Heinrich Kramer and James Sprenger, authors of a book on witchcraft, *Malleus Maleficarum* [Hammer of Witches]. As they maintained, "Witchcraft comes from carnal lust, which is in women insatiable." Their book, which detailed techniques for torturing witches (most of them women) to force them to confess, became so popular that fourteen editions were published by 1520.

The Reformation began in the sixteenth century, overlapping the Renaissance and reflecting the dynamism it had generated. It was a middle- and lower-class movement, defined primarily by its stress on individual freedom and independence. H. G. Wells viewed the Reformation as a movement motivated by three distinct groups: by the princely rulers who wanted to stop the flow of money to Rome and keep the riches and other powers for themselves; by the people opposed to the unrighteousness of the church and of the rich and powerful; and by those within the church who wanted to restore its goodness and power, for example, St. Francis of Assisi.[9]

One of the results of the Reformation was the separation of the Protestant churches from the Roman Catholic church. Another was a change in the laws regarding marriage. Martin Luther (1483–1546), the "father of the Reformation," spoke out against the traditional "sacrament" of marriage that would not allow for divorce unless approved by the church. A lusty man, Luther believed the purpose of marriage was for sex, offspring and life together with mutual fidelity. Personal growth and self-actualization were ideas that had not yet been given life.

A position similar to Luther's was taken by Martin Bucer, originally a Dominican monk. He believed in a spiritual equality in marriage and felt women should have the right to remarry if, for example, a husband was adulterous. This view was accepted in Germany, Holland, Scandinavia, and Scotland in the seventeenth century, but did not gain approval in England until two hundred years later.

John Calvin, a less human "reformer" than his predecessors, claimed that "all companionship outside of marriage between a man and a woman is damned. . . . Marriage has been given to us in order to bridle our lust. Couples are warned and commanded not to pollute the relationship with unbridled and self-indulgent lust."[10] Marriage, in Calvin's view, certainly had no room for fun, joy, or sensuality. Some people still believe Calvin was right.

The pursuit of happiness in the New World

Some of the restrictive practices of the Old World were carried to the New World by its early settlers. For example, John Calvin's dogmatic condemnation of sexual pleasure and emphasis on hard work dominated the minds of many who came, especially the Puritans. Their antisexual and moralistic views were rooted in the ancient Roman law, on which English common law was based. This code prevailed in the colonies; consequently, wives were allowed many duties but few rights. They could not own property or sign a contract, and a husband could restrain his wife and require her to submit sexually and to live where and as he chose.

During the early settlement period, marriage again was often undertaken for convenience and companionship. The prevailing religious view was that marriage should be secondary to religious life, so that there would be no danger of idolizing a spouse. Sexual delight in marriage was also supposed to be subordinate to the tasks of rearing children and "doing the work of the Lord."

Yet freedom was on the move. New land, new social groupings, and new chances to move up the many available ladders to success motivated early pioneers and settlers to shed the shackles of tradition in many areas. In the 1630s Anne Hutchinson was the first woman in the New World to question the subordinate role of women and their lack of freedom in marriage. Though she and some of her followers were killed as a consequence of their activism, the cause of equality was carried on by others, notably Abigail Adams.

Abigail, wife of John Adams, who later became the second president of the United States, believed English common law should be changed to permit women to have equal rights under the Constitution. She was angry at taxation without representation and noted this same unfairness in marriage, an institution that served primarily the needs of men. She wrote to her husband in 1777, threatening:

> *In the new code of laws which I suppose it will be necessary for you to make, I desire you would remember the ladies and be more generous and favorable to them than your ancestors. Do not put such unlimited power into the hands of the husbands. Remember, all men would be tyrants if they could. If particular care and attention is not paid to the ladies, we are determined to foment a rebellion, and will not hold ourselves bound by any laws in which we have no voice or representation.*[11]

In spite of the courage and efforts of Abigail Adams and others like her, it has taken decades for women to gain substantial rights in their lives and in their marriages. In fact, marriage is still highly restrictive in many parts of the world. In some cultures, marriage remains a strictly arranged affair. Recently, Saudi Arabian Princess Misha and her commoner husband were executed because she married outside the royal family. The king did not kill her himself, but allowed his brother to sign the death order. She was shot to death in front of her husband; he was then beheaded.

As women in the United States gained more rights—first with the suffrage movement and then with the increasing impetus of the feminist movement—marriage began to change dramatically. Today, more and more women are choosing to work, while more and more men are assuming at least some of the child-rearing responsibilities. The institution of marriage itself is being questioned and many couples live together instead of marrying. Other couples use their new-found freedom in creative ways—to foster individual growth while still committing themselves to a lifelong, loving marriage.

Freedom from, freedom to

Clearly, history and tradition have strongly shaped and continue to influence many of our current beliefs about marriage. Just as our cultures have moved toward more and more freedom, so has the institution of marriage and so have we as individuals. In fact, the idea of individualism has gained such sway that many couples choose divorce if they believe their "freedom" has been thwarted by their marriages. "I need space . . . I need my freedom" is a common theme of today's marital dialogues.

Freedom is a powerful word. It implies a growing process toward self-actualization. Erich Fromm believes that, although we as individuals have increasingly freed ourselves from many of the external political forces that control our lives, we have also been afraid of that freedom and have thus chosen new kinds of enslavement, psychological parallels to the authoritarian governments we fought to be free from in the past.[12]

Throughout history marriage has often been literally a form of enslavement or a trap. Today, ironically, many couples enslave *themselves*—to television, to a workaholic environment, or to the frantic search for "fun" that takes so many forms. These people are not free. They are oppressive to themselves and others.

Because of our new focus on individualism, few couples think of marriage as an institution that can permit and promote freedom to discover a dynamic form of human existence, one in which they can live actively and spontaneously and be with—and for—each other.

To my knowledge, freedom has not yet been used to demonstrate the potential for *couples* who happen to be married. It has only been used for individuals. I find it personally exciting to think this way. Today many couples are free from the old dawn-to-dark jobs that left them too physically exhausted to pursue much else. They now have freedom to design their own lives, to use their leisure time in creative ways, to be "couple-actualized" as well as self-actualized.

This new sense of freedom was recognized by a middle-aged couple who had lived together for a year and then decided to get married very simply. When asked by their friends why they didn't want more of a celebration, they explained, "We don't want to *get* married, we want to *be* married. This is what we are dedicated to. We're committing ourselves to this future and we intend to work on it for the rest of our lives. That will probably take courage. We may fight and disagree at times, but we're not kids living in a Romeo and Juliet world of fantasy. We used to be when we were young. No more, and thank goodness. At last we're *free* of that stuff. Our love and commitment to marriage has freed us. We haven't 'done it ourselves', as they say in some therapy groups, and we didn't do it to each other. It's our new focus. Our need is to live out a marriage of commitment."

Chapter 3

"Sometimes I wonder why we got married."

"What do you mean?"

"Well, in the beginning you seemed so interested in me."

"I still am."

"How come you always put the children first?"

"Well, I have to. They need me."

"I need you too, honey."

"Do you really? After all this time?"

"I sure do. I still get a thrill thinking of you."

The Five Views of Marriage

Getting married is easy for many people. Staying married is also easy for many. But staying married *and* being happy is not so easy. It takes motivation; it takes courage; it takes awareness. Happily married couples accomplish important tasks. They learn how to live together, how to give and take and compromise, how to keep that essential spark of excitement burning, and how to solve problems.

As noted in Chapter 2, perspectives and ideas of marriage have changed from century to century. In this chapter, the focus is on the five basic views of marriage that have developed throughout history: marriage for convenience, for a spiritual union, for romance, for companionship, and for loving.

Sometimes each partner has a different notion of what marriage should be all about. When partners differ, the relationship may be a growing, dynamic one—or it may be angry and full of conflict. When both husband and wife share a similar view of marriage, their relationship may be comfortable and empathetic—or it may become merely routine. Learning how to identify attitudes toward marriage and how to use these insights for a loving marriage is the goal of this chapter.

Although there are probably as many ways to characterize marriage as there are married people, most of these views essentially fall into one of the five categories that have developed over the course of history:

Marriage for convenience. Historically, most marriages were ones of convenience. And it is apparent that many people *still* marry for reasons of convenience—for a sexual partner, for financial security, to have a family, or simply because "that's what you're supposed to do."

Marriage for spiritual union. One couple expressed this view with, "Our marriage must have been made in heaven. It seems as though God brought us together." Spiritual marriages can be based on common religious views or on a mystical communion the couple feels is present in their relationship.

Marriage for romance. Eternal passion, knights in white armour, and the overcoming of seemingly insurmountable obstacles to join one's beloved are what come to mind when we talk of romance. The romantic view of marriage is often the stuff of movies and novels.

Marriage of companionship. People who marry for companionship are more interested in being friends than in being lovers. They often share similar interests and ambitions and hold their mutual affection dear.

Marriage for loving. Some people choose a loving marriage as a life-style. One woman explained, "We have to work at it, but it's worth the struggle. We're like a team with the same goals. A marriage for loving takes a lot of intense loving to make it work out right. We have to concentrate on it."

Some marriages include, to varying degrees, elements of all five views. Other marriages focus exclusively on one. In still others, one partner may view marriage one way, while the other has a quite different perspective.

It is not uncommon for couples to change their views of marriage from time to time. A changing attitude is often related to personal growth, advancing age, crisis, serious illness, or awareness that other possibilities exist for the marriage. For example, two people who marry in a romantic fever, with stars in their eyes and dreams in their hearts, may later find their marriage evolving into one of convenience or simply companionship. Alternatively, couples who marry for financial convenience or psychological support may find, to their surprise, that marriage is actually for loving.

Marriage for convenience

People who marry for convenience often view their union as a "practical solution" to a specific problem. Historically the oldest reason for marriage, convenience took many forms: political, family, economic, psychological, sexual, and so forth. Even in the recent past, the rugged life of the farmer made it imperative for him to have as much help as possible in working the fields and bringing in the harvest. A wife and many children were not only a convenience—they were a necessity. Arranged marriages of offspring were frequently advantageous for the parents. They could marry off a child they couldn't afford or gain a dowry or another pair of hands to help out in the family business. Often a new son-in-law or daughter-in-law offered parents the assurance that someone would take care of them in their declining years.

Today people still marry for convenience, although their reasons for doing so may differ from those of their ancestors. Some contemporary marriages are motivated by a sense of *social convenience* or social conformity. Many people find it more convenient and more comfortable to comply with what's expected of them than to live an alternative life-style. So they get married. "Everyone I know is getting married. I don't want to be an oddball." "I never even thought about it. I just always knew that I'd go to college, get married, and have a family."

Often a young man or woman will reach an age when most of their friends are getting married and will feel the need to do likewise. It may not matter that the right mate hasn't yet appeared. In the rush not to be left behind, a person may see the current dating partner as a better choice than he or she actually is. This is often a mistake.

People also marry for *psychological convenience.* They may want to take care of someone—or be taken care of. Knowingly or unknowingly they select a partner who fills the expected role. If one decides later in the marriage not to play "helpless" or "helpful," the marriage may change for the better—or it may disintegrate. Psychological convenience takes another form as well: some individuals cannot bear to be alone and so marry out of fear or anxiety. The person who often feels confused and inadequate is likely to be drawn to a decision maker.

> *Daphne was the kind of person who liked to be supportive of people. She was friendly and outgoing, unfailingly effervescent at parties. Collin, a quiet but serious young junior executive, married Daphne, probably without realizing he was doing so because she would "shine" for both of them at his company's social functions.*

Sexual convenience is another strong motivation for getting married. Although some people prefer the excitement of a variety of sexual partners and the thrill of chance encounters, many others prefer a predictable and steady source of sexual fulfillment. They have no interest in the continual search for a potential sexual partner. They want to be sure they have one.

Because of strong religious or family sanctions against premarital sex, some people who experience sex drives "impossible to control" get married just so they can have sex conveniently and in an acceptable framework. They may feel pressured by their own urges, or they may feel pressured by someone who says, "I won't go to bed with you until we're married." Rather than give into the sexual pressures, they succumb to the social ones.

Family convenience may be the force that brings people together. If a woman becomes pregnant out of wedlock, the couple may get married to avoid social disapproval or to "give the baby a name," so it will not be considered illegitimate. It has been estimated that one out of every five first-born children in the United States is conceived before marriage; obviously marriage for family convenience is not uncommon.

Many young couples who live together today do not get married unless pregnancy occurs. Then they marry out of choice, not out of fear or compulsion. Other couples get married because they deeply love and want children and believe it's more convenient to have them in a marriage framework than outside of one. Having a family is a high priority and they want to provide a stable home for their hoped-for children.

Single parents remarry after divorce or the death of a spouse for family convenience. They want partners to parent their children, so that their offspring will not miss the "advantages" of family life. These hoped-for advantages may include help with discipline, finances, repairing things around the house, doing the laundry, preparing the meals, providing affection, and so on. It is often difficult and lonely to be a single parent, so for many remarriage is an attractive option.

Marriage for *economic convenience* happens in many ways. Two persons who are wealthy may want to meld their fortunes, or one person may have property or access to money and the other wants it. In a morganatic[1] marriage, designed to protect a family fortune from exploitation, the bride gives up all rights to her husband's estate for herself and her children. However, it is not necessary for one or the other partner to be wealthy for a marriage to be one of economic convenience. A person with a steady paycheck, even a moderate one, often has great appeal.

Marriages of retired older people often are economically motivated. If one person has a pension, and the other has Social Security, they might manage better together than alone. Until recent legislation, some older persons who were living on Social Security retirement checks decided to live together for companionship without marriage, since that would reduce the amount of their checks and impose an unnecessary economic burden on them.

Economic convenience is often tied in to the *type* of partner one selects. A corporation employee who aspires to move ahead professionally may marry someone who fits the corporate image of what a spouse "should" be. A minister's spouse is often crucial in the kind of church assignments he or she receives. Life insurance companies, when hiring a male employee, may interview the individual's wife, so that they can assess her ability to be supportive of his work and her willingness to spend many long evenings alone when he is out selling policies.

Often economic convenience will keep a marriage intact although neither partner may be happy. One of my clients tells this story:

> *I've fallen in love with someone else. She wants me to get a divorce and marry her. But my wife would really take me to the laundry. By the time she was done with the divorce, I wouldn't have a dime. I've decided that I just don't want to give up all that money. So I'm going to stay married.*

Royal marriages were often born of *political convenience*—the joining together of clans, lands, fortunes, and often most importantly, military strength. Royal advisors spent a great deal of time working out a marriage that would establish just the right military or political alliances. Often the bride and groom were merely pawns in a power game; frequently their first meeting was not until the wedding.

Immigration to a place of safety or to avoid oppression is a more common reason today for a marriage of political convenience. Because of immigration quotas, marriage to a citizen of another country is sometimes the only way to escape the terrorism or poverty of one's native land. Immigration is more of a possibility for people who are married to a citizen of the country they wish to emigrate to. For example, many citizens of Communist bloc countries, who desire to move to the free West, must first go to Communist East Germany, where they actually advertise for a marriage of convenience. A common newspaper classified ad reads:

> *Foreigner wants woman for marriage.*
> *No obligations on her part.*
> *Purpose: to get residence permit.*[2]

Marriages for convenience, which originally developed out of very basic survival needs, still have value. Today, it is still convenient to know who will "bring home the bacon" and who will "wash up the mess." It is still convenient to have a warm body to snuggle up to and a source of sexual satisfaction—whether in a cold house, a tent, or under the stars. It is still convenient to be able to rely on spoken or unspoken assumptions about who will do what and when they will do it.

Marriages of convenience provide practical solutions to very real problems. Such marriages may remain stable and strong as long as the relationship remains "convenient" in some way to both partners. When each acts according to implicit or explicit premarital expectations—for example, "you mow the lawn and I'll clean the house"—the convenience continues. Sometimes these marriages include elements of romanticism or companionship. Sometimes they develop into loving relationships.

Spiritual marriage

For many centuries people have searched for words to describe the concept "spiritual." The Egyptians used the word *Ka* to denote the transcendent part of a person, that which is neither mind nor body. The Hebrews used *nephesh,* meaning "breath." The Greeks used the word *psyche,* which can be translated as "soul" or "mind."

Although some philosophies deny the existence of a spiritual component in human beings, there is today a ground-swell movement to recognize the spiritual part of a person, even if this element is not easily defined or readily understood. People are turning to meditation, prayer, parapsychology, and holistic health to get in touch with their inner selves and with the peace that often accompanies that process. For me, the spiritual part of the self is a reality, the inner core of a person's being. It is capable of transcendence in many forms. Perhaps it is immortal. It is surely the essence of a person.

I use the term *spiritual* to describe a relationship in which people's innermost selves—those selves that transcend their daily external selves—meet and relate. In some marriages where this happens, the communion is an unspoken occurrence; the partners may feel they are "on the same wavelength" or receiving "good karma" from each other. In other cases, the individuals may feel that they knew each other in a previous existence or were destined to meet and marry because of their spiritual paths.

Instead of using the word *spiritual,* some couples use a related word, *sacrament.* The word comes from the early Christian church and essentially means

holy and mysterious. A sacrament is a tangible token signifying and conveying God's love and grace. A sacrament, therefore, makes something sacred. In this there is a mystery, "a visible sign of what is invisible."

One of the early stories of the sacramental view of marriage has this quality of mystery. It comes from the Bible and is about a wedding in Cana. When the wine ran out, Jesus is said to have turned water that was to be used for purification rites into more wine (John 2:1–11). This story was used by the early Christian church to demonstrate the sacramental nature of marriage.

The concept of marriage as sacramental was initially based on the earlier Hebrew idea of covenant. The Hebrews saw themselves as having a covenant with God—God would watch over them as His "chosen people" if they observed His laws and were faithful to Him. Thus marriage, being a religious covenant, usually required exclusiveness and faithfulness for life.

In the Roman Catholic church, wedding ceremonies are currently called sacraments. In the Protestant churches they are not. Some people view all of marriage, not just the ceremony, as sacramental, because of their marriage vows and the actual experience of the wedding. They may speak of themselves as having a "sacred relationship" or say, "We took sacred promises when we got married."

Those who believe in the Judaeo-Christian tradition often feel that God is mysteriously a part of their marriage. They may make a distinction between body, mind, and spirit and emphasize the spiritual aspect. In contrast to the doctrines preached in the early Christian era, many people with religious beliefs today feel it is God's will to marry and have children.

Couples with a church background who have a sacramental view of marriage work hard to make their marriages successful. They may accept unhappiness, frustration, even brutality. They may refuse to consider divorce as a valid option. Instead they tend to "pray about it." If they let their minds wander to the possibility of divorce, they may experience strong feelings of guilt for even thinking such thoughts. A spiritual relationship has a dynamism to it that is not easily destroyed.

Many couples who do not hold traditional religious views of marriage still seek a spiritual dimension or union. They may write their own marriage vows, reflecting their belief in some form of cosmic power, which they may or may not call God. They may also include words and actions intended to celebrate the indescribable mystery of finding a spiritual dimension in all of life, because they have found themselves in each other.

Marriage as a spiritual relationship may be *unexpectedly* experienced at the moment the couple exchange their vows. This moment may be one of depth—soul to soul, spirit to spirit. Or it may be one of height—a peak experience. Psychologist Abraham Maslow describes a peak experience as one in which the whole universe is perceived as an integrated and unified whole.[3] This can be so profound as to radically change a person's character. When this occurs, a wedding has a spiritual dimension, whether or not it is called a sacrament.

Nietzsche once defined people as animals who can make promises. To me, this seems an incomplete definition. People make sacred promises because they trust themselves to keep them, because they trust a higher power for help, and because they trust that the person they make promises to is also worth trusting. They may willingly take sacred vows to be married, "till death do us part" or, as is sometimes the practice in the Mormon temple, for eternity.

Romantic marriage

Romance is idealized love. Often it is being in love with love, an infatuation spurred on by intense, erotic feelings that are delightfully exciting. Infatuation sometimes grows into love, but it can also remain simple infatuation. When people are in the throes of a romantic involvement, they may not be able to sleep, eat, or work. Like Romeo and Juliet, they may contemplate or even commit suicide if kept apart. Romanticism may be likened to a manic-depressive state, as the lovers plunge from highs of excitement to lows of despair—and back again. The Greeks viewed this phase of love as a form of mania, and Ortega y Gassett comments on it as a temporary state of imbecility.[4]

Romanticism is widely promoted on TV, in movies, and in popular "true love" magazines. It is exciting because of its melodrama. When people are infatuated, in love with love, they find great satisfaction in gazing deeply into each other's eyes or in talking for hours on the phone. They often develop a secret code—words of endearment, gestures, or facial expressions that have special romantic, often sexual, meanings.

Romanticism frequently starts with a strong physical attraction for someone and an exaggerated perception of the person's beauty or other external characteristics. Actor Richard Burton describes his physical attraction for Elizabeth Taylor when he first viewed her lying beside a swimming pool:

> *She was the most astonishing, self-contained, pulchritudinous, remote, inaccessible woman I had ever seen. Her breasts were apocalyptic, they would topple empires down before they were withered.*[5]

Romanticism may also start with a fantasized exaggeration of a person's skills or intellect. Sometimes this initial attraction for a person's breasts, thighs, wit, or intelligence diminishes in intensity as the novelty wears off. Without something more to hold people together, a marriage may collapse.

In the past, romantic love was not considered to be a part of marriage. As we noted in Chapter 2, courtiers and knights of the Middle Ages were only duty-bound to their spouses and reserved their passion and adoration for other ladies of the court. Their romantic love involved self-torture and suffering; sexual desire was restrained and thus stoked into fiery passion. (The word *passion* comes from the root "to suffer.") Often an obstacle separated the two lovers. Whether it was a feat the knight had to achieve to win the favor of his beloved or a chastity belt that kept a relationship unconsummated, the obstacle kept the infatuation at a feverish high.

This notion of love may be viewed as the historical basis of our current romantic ideas of love and marriage. Anyone who has ever experienced infatuation and strong sexual attraction no doubt remembers the ecstacy of anticipating a possible meeting or a clandestine embrace, as well as the agonies of separation. In romantic love, attraction grows stronger when those involved are separated physically or when other obstacles—for example, family opposition—intervene. Parents may refuse to accept the person their son or daughter claims to be in love with. Or perhaps the armed services, a commitment to

finish school, or a faraway job may require separation. Lack of money, conflicting values, different religions, or being married to someone else are other hurdles.

Romanticism takes different forms, wears different faces, and uses different words throughout the world and over the centuries. Yet the elements remain constant: idealized exaggeration of the other person's qualities, obstacles to the marriage, and often geographical distance between the two who see themselves so desperately "in love." When obstacles to the union no longer exist and marriage becomes possible or a reality, the excitement may fade.

It is not unusual for married couples who enter into marriage with this attitude to later complain that "there's no romance left" or that "the glow is gone.'' The phrase ''the honeymoon is over'' signifies the end of a period of romantic infatuation and a decrease in the ''fever'' that brought such a mingling of delight and agony when obstacles seemed so difficult and suffering so intense. This was expressed by a couple who came for marriage counseling. ''Actually,'' they claimed, ''we have what we need financially, but *the excitement has gone* ever since we got married. Our marriage is just plain boring. What happened?''

Being in love with a person is quite different from being in love with love. The romance in loving a person involves recognizing and treating that person as someone special and wonderful—but *not* as someone adored or idealized. Romance is for real; romanticism is not.

Marriage for companionship

Whereas purely romantic marriages thrive on heavenly daydreams and hellish agonies, marriages for companionship are much more down-to-earth. Instead of face-to-face (but sometimes blind) adoration, partners who are companions walk side-by-side. Albert Camus expresses it well:

> *Don't walk in front of me,*
> *I may not follow.*
> *Don't walk behind me,*
> *I may not lead.*
> *Walk beside me,*
> *And just be my friend.*

The word *companion* originally meant one ''who eats bread with another,'' *com* meaning together and *panis* meaning bread. Currently, however, the word is used in a wider context. ''I don't care if she does have some problems, she's fun to be married to.'' ''So what if he's not perfect, he listens when I talk to him.'' ''We have a lot of interests in common, more so than most people.'' ''Actually we don't have sex often, but we're friends.''

In all of these comments, the emphasis is on compatible ideals, interests, or tasks. Similar tastes, such as music or art, or mutually enjoyed activities, such as tennis and gardening, are prerequisites. The marriage is regarded more as a partnership than as a romantic liaison or as an intense love relationship. Although the two persons are not always together, do not always agree, and do not necessarily engage in the same activities, they find pleasure in the interests

they have in common and they respect each other's unique interests. These relationships usually include elements of convenience and often grow into loving marriages.

Marriage for companionship is often preferred when romance per se is not valued, when sex is either not enjoyed or is seen as distasteful or evil, or when sexual desires decrease because of illness or other factors.

As people grow older, companionship seems to be more important to them than any other element of marriage. Having a mate to talk to, to cry with, to care for—to just help keep the wolf of loneliness away from the door—is a high priority for older persons. Thus, a marriage of companionship might grow out of mutual needs.

This is true for others as well. Many young couples first live together and then choose to get married as they discover the freedom and growth that are possible in friendship. They are comrades in a very real sense and will support each other against the world if need be. For some of these people, sexual involvement or romantic moments are less important than their friendship; they like each other's company for other reasons. When they marry, they have a strong foundation on which to build their future relationship.

Being friends in a companionship marriage can be the most liberating relationship possible, because friendships are not defined by society or law, only by the two people involved. Companionship marriages are usually sound ones; however, either or both partners may look outside the relationship for excitement. Sometimes this excitement takes the form of an intense interest in, say, politics or bridge or gardening or a job. Sometimes it means an extramarital affair. So-called open marriages occur most often within marriages for companionship, because there is a low level of possessiveness.

> *Friendship's cement is the freedom to be, not just to do. The words "friend" and "free" grew out of each other. The Old English word* freo *meant free; not in bondage; noble; glad. The Old English word* freon *means to love, and the word* freoud *becomes our modern English "friend."*[6]

Marriage is for loving

People talk about love in many ways. They say they are "falling in love" or "out of love." They speak of "making love" or "losing love." They express the love they feel for their family or friends. All of these forms of love are valid, but are not the focus of this book. Love as used here will be considered solely within the framework of marriage.

I am totally convinced that love creates love in people who care about each other *in any way at all.* Even if their caring takes the disguised form of a marriage for sexual or economic convenience, I believe caring people have the potential to create a marriage that is for loving. Loving is life-giving, it is healing, it provides freedom and releases energy. It is intense. It is durable. It is without exploitation. It is worth fighting for, maybe worth dying for, and definitely worth living for.

Definitions both clarify and confuse. Some books that define love quote the Sanskrit word *lubhyati,* which means "he desires." Others use Greek derivatives such as *eros* and *agape.* Webster says it's "a feeling of strong personal attachment induced by sympathetic understanding or by ties of kinship; ardent affection."

What I mean by "love" is enchantment, desire, and unconditional good will. People in love are able to express meaningful emotions to one another, directly and openly, without ulterior motives. Love has sparkle and pleasure; it generates ardent affection and strong physical attraction. It sometimes has highs; it sometimes has lows. Underneath both feelings usually flows a steady current of trust and appreciation for oneself and for one's partner.

To love actively is to experience tenderness, to hold dear, to desire, to esteem, to trust, to believe in. Words such as affection, attachment, fondness, or devotion do not carry the intensity or depth of feeling conveyed by the word *love.* Freud said love was an attachment, not a feeling, yet people are often attached to those they do not even like.

Love wants the best for the other, without stopping to question, "What's in it for me?" Sometimes the loved one is more important than oneself. In 1936 Edward VIII of Britain abdicated the throne to marry Wallis Simpson. It was reported that he "gave up everything" for the woman he loved. On the contrary, he seemed to have recognized the infinite gains of a truly loving relationship.

Love in marriage is often more intense than in other relationships. It is centered on a particular person—it bonds the inner core of one to the inner core of another. Love looks beyond externals to the inner self of one's mate.

Sometimes closeness and intimacy arise from everyday concerns, like a child's illness or a financial problem. Then the element of convenience may also be

present. Sometimes the closeness is linked with a peak experience, and a sense of sacrament is felt by both partners. Sometimes the closeness accompanies a delightful evening of candles, flowers, and wine—and the couple rediscovers romance, even romanticism. Sometimes the closeness comes with a shared book, a walk in the rain, or an evening of music—and a marriage of companionship is enjoyed.

Active loving Each of these attitudes is present from time to time when the people involved know that marriage is for loving. Loving is an active word. Therefore, a loving marriage involves some give-and-take for the convenience of each other, some sacramental experiences of transcendent beauty, some romantic moments of exciting passion, some common interests and the non-possessiveness of lasting friendship. These are the things that cement a marriage, that create oneness and allow for separateness. A loving marriage can have them all.

The strongest marriages seem to be those in which all five views of marriage are recognized, expressed, and woven together in a beautiful tapestry. Novelist Nathaniel Hawthorne expressed this well when he wrote of his wife: "We met in Eternity, and there our intimacy was formed. My wife is, in the strictest sense, my sole companion, and I need no other. There is no vacancy in my mind any more than in my heart."[7]

Loving can become a life-style when people respond with their minds, their bodies, and their spiritual selves. Some people avoid loving in this way. They may be afraid of losing their individuality, afraid their intensity may turn a spiritual relationship into an idolatrous one, or afraid they will be exploited in some way. Thus they are afraid to be ardent, afraid to be intensely involved, afraid to let themselves go. Their fear of becoming vulnerable stands in the way of their experiencing oneness. They're missing a lot.

After ten years of a rather stormy marriage in which oneness didn't live up to their expectations, Carole left a note for Bill on the mirror he used when shaving:

> *I want you to change some of the things you do and say to me* and *I'll love you even if you don't because I love you for who you are, not just for what you do. Often I don't even like what you do, Bill, but I love you. Does this make sense?*

Bill sent back a note to her:

> *I'm glad you like me and who I am, because if you didn't, there's no point to this marriage. I don't like feeling as if I have to perform for you, Carole. I just want to be me. When I am* me *and you like me, then I can and I want to change, so that things will get better.*

Things do get better when couples love each other for their uniqueness, not just for convenience, for romance, for companionship, or as a spiritual mate. "For better or worse, for richer or poorer, in sickness and in health . . . I love you." This is unconditional loving.

Chapter 4

"Our marriage isn't what I expected."

"It's not for me, either."

"We have such different ideas."

"We sure do. You and your snobbish Back Bay Boston ancestors!"

"How about those lace curtain Irish ancestors of *yours*?"

"No wonder we fight!"

"We each think, 'I'm right and you're wrong'."

"Well, I still love you, even if your ancestors did come over on the Mayflower."

"I still love you, too, you old Son of Killarny, you!"

You and Your Marriage: The Past

Every marriage has a past. The past of your marriage is not only rooted in your childhood, in your experiences with your family and with other families; the roots are deeper than that. They go back in time, back to previous generations and different cultures, when life-styles were very different, and views of marriage were also different.

The family past

We cannot disown our roots. Our ancestors and their habits, principles, and hang-ups are part of us. We are who we are partly because of where we came from. Knowingly or unknowingly we have been affected by our past history. The past of any marriage can have major or minor effects on the present.

> *One young couple who came for counseling faced a severe crisis because of their cultural differences. He was of German descent; she was Japanese. At Christmas he wanted a feast with all the German foods that were part of his tradition. After three years of trying unsuccessfully to please him with her cooking, she felt depressed and insecure. "Will we ever be able to get our differences together?" she lamented.*

Traditions that are upheld, expected roles that are played out, ideas about the purpose of marriage, how to raise children, even foods that are served, are often holdovers from the past. For example, many couples when getting married want food for the wedding that reflects their past. Often food has symbolic connections with fertility. Salted cream with sugar is an old Netherlands custom that symbolizes the bitter and sweet parts of marriage. The same idea is represented with English wedding cake with bitter almonds and sugar icing. Unmarried girls going to the wedding would save a piece to put under their pillows, hoping to thus dream of their own future husbands. The use of rice to shower a couple is a symbolic reference to fertility; so, too, is the showering of a Jewish couple with wheat or barley, along with the call, "Be fruitful and multiply," said three times.

Even a simple action such as holding hands in public can be linked to family history. My family was of English descent, responsible, hardworking, with a built-in reserve and dislike for "showing emotions in public." Members of my husband's family were quite different. They openly showed feelings of affection. As a result, he was, and still is, a sentimental romanticist.

When I first knew him I was very surprised when he commented favorably about a couple sitting on a park bench, holding hands and looking lovingly at each other. I thought to myself, "Surely he doesn't approve of *that* in public." But he did.

I began to think about it and asked myself, "Why not?" And when I couldn't come up with a legitimate reason *why not,* I changed, and I enjoyed becoming more impulsive and affectionate myself. Once I realized my bias was based on a cultural holdover and not on conscious reason, it was a delight to release my own "sentimental romanticism."

Festivity and fantasy

Clearly, the past continues to affect the present. Viewpoints about the purpose of marriage, family, and cultural traditions are often passed on from one generation to another. These viewpoints may enrich a marriage or they may create problems.

I believe that people need to study and celebrate the past, just as they need to fantasize and plan for the future. The present is the intersection of past and future. It is important, but it is only one part of the whole. Our capacity for festivity and fantasy may wither away if we live only in the present.

Fantasy is usually future-oriented. In contrast, festivity, according to theologion Harvey Cox,[1] is basically related to the past. It is almost always a celebration of an event that has occurred. Anniversaries, birthdays, religious and national holidays—all are opportunities for festivities. People who cut themselves off from celebrations and festivity may feel themselves cut off without roots.

This chapter is in two parts. The first part includes discovery exercises to help you recall events and feelings in your life and marriage that can be recognized and perhaps grieved for or celebrated with festivity and joy.

The second part of the chapter introduces Transactional Analysis, a theory for understanding people, how they got to be the way they are, and how they relate to others. This theory, often called TA, is one of the best tools you can use to evaluate yourself and your marriage.

TA includes several subtheories, and this will show you how to use two of them—the theory of personality and the theory of life scripts—to evaluate the effect of your past on your present marriage. Two later chapters, "You and Your Marriage: The Present" and "You and Your Marriage: The Future," will use other subtheories of Transactional Analysis. TA is not difficult to learn. It is interesting, often fun, and, most important, it works!

As you work on this chapter keep the five views of marriage in mind. Remember that marriage is often for convenience. It can also be a spiritual union, a torrid romance, or a friendly companionship. All of these are possible when marriage is for loving. By the time you finish this chapter, you will know how you arrived at your basic views and traditions. You will have a fairly complete "history" of your marriage.

First Impressions

What happens to any marriage is often related to first impressions. The fact that people often dress up to apply for a job or go to a party where there will be strangers is clear indication that they believe first impressions are important and often lasting.

Appearance. One of the things I used to observe first in men was their hands. If they looked strong and muscular, I fantasized that the man could protect me. If they looked long and slender, I assumed he was artistic. Of course, these judgments were made on the basis of little evidence. Strong hands could brutalize instead of protect, and long, slender hands could just as easily belong to a scientist or accountant as to an artist. Like me, you may have observed people's appearance first. On the basis of how they look (shoulders, breasts, legs, hair, clothes, eyes, and so on), you may conclude, "Yes, I do like that person," or, "No, I don't."

> What was your first impression of the person you married? What did you think about his/her appearance? How did you feel?

Actions. When I was trying to decide whether or not to marry my present husband, who had been divorced and had four almost-grown children, I carefully observed how they acted toward one another. Because my own children are very important to me, I was certain that anyone I married would need to feel the same way about his. I observed that this man and his children were open, honest, affectionate, warm, and fun-loving with each other. And I was greatly attracted by this. I guessed our values about the importance of children would be compatible.

> What actions of your partner attracted you? Did any actions turn you off? Did your partner act differently after you got to know him/her better?

Words. "I love you" is still what most people long to hear. Other words may imply "I love you" and be just as effective. On our first date, my future husband must have intuited what I wanted. He requested a dance orchestra to play "I'll Take Care of Your Cares for You." I interpreted these words to mean "I love you and we'll live happily ever after." Since then, we have often taken turns "taking care" of each other in one way or another.

How about you? What words were used? How did you interpret them?

Flashback to Childhood

Early childhood experiences with marriage are important because they shape our later views and attitudes toward marriage. When you were young . . .

What did you observe about your parents' marriage?

How they expressed affection

How they spent money

How they made decisions

How they used leisure time

Other elements of their marriage

How has this affected your own ideas about marriage?

What did your mother say about

Whom to marry

When to marry

What marriage would be like

What did your father and other parental figures say about

Whom to marry

When to marry

What marriage would be like

Are you living your marriage on the basis of what you learned in childhood?

When First We Met

Sit down in a quiet, comfortable place. Take a few deep, slow breaths. Relax your feet, legs, body, shoulders, arms, hands, and face. Let your mind float back into the past . . . to when you first met the person you married or might be planning on marrying.

> *See* again the total environment: where you were, the occasion, who was there, and what everyone was doing.
>
> *Listen* to the sounds that you once heard, the words of introduction, voices of other people speaking to you, and perhaps the background noises or background music.
>
> *Experience* once more the initial attraction, indifference, or distaste. These first impressions may have become important in your marriage.
>
> Let your other senses explore the past. Can you still *taste* something you tasted then? Still feel the first *touch* of the other person? Is there anything you can still *smell,* such as perfume or shaving lotion or body scent?
>
> Stay with the experience for at least ten minutes.

Chasing vs. Courting

Chasing and courting are two different things. Chasing the unobtainable or almost unobtainable is often the major excitement before marriage. As one wife said, "I wanted him because so many other women were after him." If a chase ends in marriage, it usually becomes one of convenience—sexually and psychologically.

Courting, on the other hand, has an element of romance. It stresses the importance of developing companionship, a time to find out whether two people are emotionally and sexually compatible. Sometimes a courtship occurs long after the marriage. When a couple decides to become friends after years of resentments, they sometimes have to learn how to court each other. This may be a new skill or one that has become rusty with disuse.

> Let your mind drift back to the first time you were "chased" by someone and the first time you "chased" someone else or wanted to.
>
> What did your experiences with successful chasing lead to?

How did you feel after an unsuccessful experience with chasing?

In your own life, which has been more effective—the adolescent chase or the romantic wooing and courting?

Was it chasing or courting that led to your marriage?

The Courtship Process

Some people have long courtships that last for years. Others meet and decide almost immediately that they can't wait to get married. They are in a hurry, often experiencing high excitement and pressure to get married. Here is a time line ending in marriage on which you can chart your own courtship. How long was it between the time you met and your wedding ceremony? Include specific events of your courtship, such as when he/she proposed, a special engagement party, any conflicts, and so on.

First meeting ____ Wedding ceremony

After charting your courtship, let other memories come into your awareness.

What my mother said about the courtship ______________________________

What my father said about the courtship ______________________________

What my friends said about the courtship ______________________________

Do you remember the moment you decided you wanted to marry your partner? What was happening? How did you feel?

Close your eyes and relive the moment.

Who wanted to get married first? Who proposed first? What was the other's reaction? What was your reaction to that feeling?

Do you know why you wanted to get married? What views did you have then?

GOOD
LUCK

JUST
MARRIED...
AGAIN
927·01W

Daydreams from the Past

When people daydream, they let down some of their internal defenses. They allow themselves to imagine marriage creatively and to fantasize about marriage roles they might get involved in. They may "know" these creations are unrealistic, yet they are aware that at some level their daydreams have important messages for them.

> See yourself once more, before you were married. Describe one or more daydreams you had about marriage.
>
> Do your daydreams reveal anything about your basic expectations about marriage? How do you explain this to yourself?
>
> Do your expectations point to the basic views you had about what marriage should be or could be?
>
> Have your past views changed in any ways? If so, how?

The Big Event

Getting ready for the wedding, the ceremony itself, and the events that immediately follow are sometimes joyful, sometimes not. The purpose of this exercise is to clarify similar or dissimilar likes and dislikes. Let your mind drift back to the past; then fill in the following columns.

Getting ready for the wedding ceremony

	Preparing for the wedding	*During the wedding*	*After the wedding*
I liked	____________	____________	____________
My partner liked	____________	____________	____________
I disliked	____________	____________	____________
My partner disliked	____________	____________	____________

Look at your above lists. On a scale of 1 to 10 (with 10 being high), how would you rate the wedding from your perspective? How might your marriage partner rate it?

Has this part of your past affected your marriage? If so, how?

Sex: Before and After

Some people enter marriage with little or no sexual experience or education. Others have a great deal. Their experiences may be negative or positive and their sexual education may be sufficient and accurate or incomplete and erroneous.

For most people, sexual experience during childhood and adolescence is experimental—secretive and exciting. Sometimes it provides physical release; sometimes it increases physical tension. Some parents think of it as part of normal development. Others are harshly critical, and their children often develop a strong sense of guilt for even "thinking that way."

Recall some of your childhood sexual experiments and experiences. Let your memory stay with them for a few minutes, then jot a couple of them down.

My positive experiences

My parents' reactions

Others' reactions

My negative experiences

My parents' reactions

Others' reactions

Now consider how these experiences affected you during courtship and after your marriage.

The Crises

Most couples face several crises in their marriages. Sometimes things get solved, sometimes not. Using the guidelines below, describe some of the crises in your marriage, whether they are now past or are still continuing.

What happened

How I reacted

How my partner reacted

How it affected our marriage

What are some cultural traditions or historical events that may have influenced the reactions of you and your partner to these crises?

Let your imagination float back into history. What marriage crises might your ancestors have faced? How might they have responded?

Possible crises of ancestors

Possible responses

Are my responses like theirs?

The Happy Times

Think for a few moments about the happy times in your marriage. List five of them below.

1. ______________________________

2. ______________________________

3. ______________________________

4. ______________________________

5. ______________________________

Were those times happy for your partner also? What made them happy? Did they meet your expectations? Did any "past history" influence them? How about your ancestors? Take a guess about their happy times.

Possible happy times of ancestors

Possible responses

Are my responses like theirs?

What is the most recent happy time in your marriage?

Why was it so happy?

How might you create more happy times?

Our Views of Marriage

When you think about the events that led up to your marriage, the event itself, and some of the events that have happened since, you may find that one attitude has predominated throughout. Or you may find an interplay of several views. This exercise is to help you become aware of your basic views.

How and when did your marriage have elements of convenience?

How and when did your marriage have a sacramental or spiritual dimension?

How and when did you express romance in your marriage?

How and when did you experience side-by-side companionship?

How and when did your marriage include loving and open intimacy without exploitation or avoidance?

Now look over the questions again and try to answer them from your partner's point of view.

If one of the five views of marriage is lacking or almost lacking, you may want to figure out how to add it to your marriage.

Marriage as a Peak Experience

Peak experiences are the high moments of emotion. Everything seems to fall into place, to become *one*—body, mind, and spirit. When this happens in a marriage, a couple may feel as if they are outside of time and space. Time, as measured by the clock, has no meaning. The space they share seems limitless and without boundaries. Hope is higher than usual. Beauty, truth, and joy integrate the two of them.

A peak experience gives a feeling of ecstasy, a sense of saying yes—to oneself, to marriage, to the universe, and to God.

Some people do not experience peak moments in marriage because they have not yet discovered and accepted themselves as persons. In spite of that lack, they may sense the potential for transcendence.

If you have not known peak experiences, do you have any clues as to why?

If you have known peak experiences, list the times and places

How did they develop?

How were you different after the experience was over?

"How Do I Love Thee? Let Me Count the Ways"

Elizabeth Barrett Browning's sonnet has captured the hearts of lovers for more than a century. Describe the ways you have loved your partner in marriage and the ways your partner has loved you.

Ways I have loved my partner

Ways my partner has loved me

How do you feel when you study the above?

Do you note any patterns emerging? If so, what are they?

Is the current situation different from the past? For better? For worse? What might this mean?

Transactional analysis and how personality affects marriage

Transactional Analysis (TA) has proved a useful tool for many couples working to enhance their marriages. It is both a theory of personality and a theory of communications. You can use TA to understand any person or situation—including yourself and the situations you face. TA is widely used by people who want to solve problems, who want to cope more successfully, who want more joy out of life.

Psychiatrist Eric Berne originated Transactional Analysis in 1958. His theories evolved as he observed how a patient's behavior changed when a new stimulus, such as a word, gesture, or sound, entered the patient's focus. These changes involved facial expressions, tone of voice, kinds of sentences used, body movements, gestures, and even posture. The patient behaved quite differently as conditions changed, as though there were several different people inside. At times one or the other of these different inner people seemed to be in control of the person's total personality.

Berne theorized that *all* of us have different parts to our personality. He defined each part, or *ego state,* as "a consistent pattern of feeling and experience directly related to a corresponding consistent pattern of behavior."[2]

He observed that three ego states appear over and over again in everyone's personality. He called these the Parent, the Adult, and the Child. (When the capital letters P, A, and C are used, they refer to ego states. When not capitalized, they refer to actual parents, adults, and children.) The accompanying figure shows how Berne diagramed the ego states of the personality.

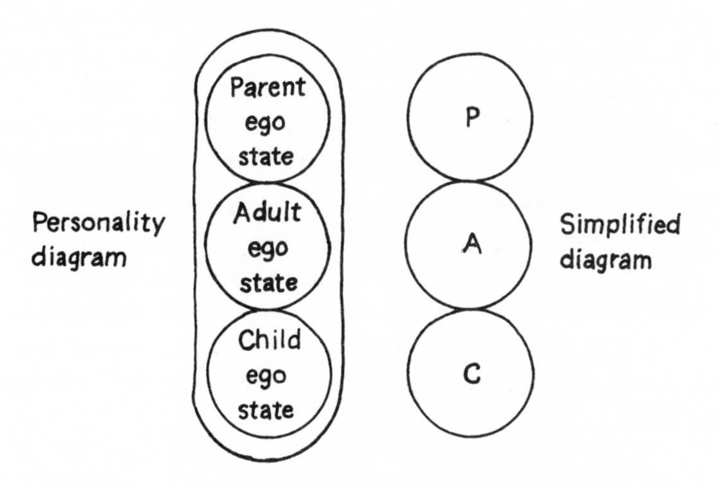

Each ego state can operate positively, for your overall welfare, or it may be operating in ways that are not loving for you. When an ego state is healthy and functioning appropriately, it enhances life and adds joy to it. Your marriage gets better. But when an ego state is overused or not allowed to operate freely, it can destroy a marriage or make it seem restrictive, unpleasant, and boring. When people have ego states that are, in part, not healthy because of past experiences, they can improve through marriage counseling, study, or some other form of personal growth.

The Parent ego state. When people are in the Parent ego state, they are feeling, thinking, and acting as their own parent figures once did. A common accusation when couples fight is, "You're just like your mother" (or father). This is not surprising, for people do act like their mothers, fathers, aunts, and uncles. When they do this, they are borrowing from the past, holding the same views about marriage and often living the same life-styles that their parents once did.

Cynthia and Joe came for marriage counseling because they disagreed strongly on how to raise their children. When first married, they were romantic, and their Child ego states were the most active. Their dream was to live happily ever after. Later, the demands of parenting their children strongly activated their Parent ego states. But often, when their energy went into their Parent ego states, they disagreed with each other. Joe demanded that the children attend a Catholic church. Cynthia said, "No way. I want them to be Baptist." The conflict between them was really a conflict between the parents they once had.

The Adult ego state. When couples are in the Adult ego state, they are *not* locked into beliefs of the past or bound by what their parents said a marriage "should" be. They are rational, tending to think clearly and exchange information. Their behavior is appropriate to the situation. Couples in the Adult ego state consider the past, plan for the future, yet live in the here and now. They analyze their marriage and the options they have for improving it.

Using the Adult ego state they work together on problems such as filing a joint income tax, balancing the budget, providing their children with a happy, stable home, discovering ways to please each other with food, music, talk, sex, and so forth. They may even explore the cost of divorce versus the cost of staying married. They have an awareness of personal values such as having a marriage partner as a close friend and lover, or believing that marriage can enrich all of life.

No one, even in the Adult ego state, has all the facts about anything, including marriage. Consequently, couples who are not aware of basic feelings and attitudes may clash unnecessarily. Information can sometimes change this situation.

The Child ego state. When people are in their Child ego state they are feeling, thinking, and acting as they did when they were little. They experience all the mixed-up feelings and inconsistent behaviors common to children. Some may want their marriage partner to be just like Mom or Dad. Or they may fear their partner, as they once did their parents. Or they may live in anticipation of the future and feel and respond on the basis of childhood daydreams.

In the Child ego state a person has a basic human urge for closeness and intimacy as well as freedom and autonomy. When the Child in a person is relatively free, that person will experience basic feelings easily. The person will be able to be creative, impulsive, intuitive, and fun, able to laugh and able to cry like a naturally free small child.

This healthy humanness is often injured psychologically in childhood by such parental comments as: "You made your bed of roses, now lie in it." Later in life a person's inner Child may still hear this command and feel unable to move out of a brutalizing marriage. A boy who hears, "A puny kid like you will never be a man," begins to believe manhood and sexuality are related to size. These kinds of childhood experiences can be reexperienced in adult life.

Sorting out ego states to understand your own personality and that of your marriage partner is important. Each ego state may have a different view of marriage. In one person, the Child ego state may prefer a romantic or psychologically convenient marriage, the Adult ego state may select an economically convenient one, and the Parent may believe in social convenience or in marriage as a sacrament. In a contemporary marriage, all three ego states may be operating simultaneously.

Traditions and Your Parent Ego State

Cultural and family traditions, life-styles, and ways of doing things are often handed down generation after generation through peoples' Parent ego states. To discuss yours, consider:

> How did your family spend holidays, celebrate birthdays, observe religious events? Did your parents have special traditions for daily living,

such as rearing children or influencing your career ("There's always been a teacher in our family")? List some of the traditions in your family and in your partner's family.

My parental traditions: ________________________________

____

____

____

____

My partner's parental traditions: ________________________________

____

____

____

____

Now compare your parental traditions with those of your spouse. Are they compatible?

If not, how do you solve your disagreements? Does one lose and the other win? Do you compromise? Do you avoid the issue?

Problem Solving and Your Adult Ego State

One of the most important functions of the Adult ego state is the ability to solve problems. Jot down a problem you had in your marriage that you were able to solve.

A problem we had in our marriage

How the problem was related to our cultural pasts

How the problem was related to our personal pasts or the past of our marriage

How we looked for ways to solve it

How we made the decision on what to do

The action we took

Our evaluation of the results

Feelings and the Child Ego State

Many people experience their strongest feelings as coming from the Child ego states. The feelings may be body-centered, whether pleasurable or painful. They may be related to dreams and expectations, again pleasureable or painful. Or they may be directly related to childhood experiences—pleasurable or painful, plus or minus.

They may say something like, "I can't stand it when you leave the house angry the way my father used to," or, "When you're sad, I feel the way I did just before Grandma died."

The purpose of this exercise is to help you trace the origins of your feelings to see how they are related to previous experiences.

Feelings I often have about my marriage

I begin to feel this way when

In childhood I sometimes felt this way when

Now think about how your marriage partner might feel. Are the Child ego states in the two of you compatible? Any changes needed? What are they?

Sex and Ego States

Sex is an important part of marriage. All couples have opinions, ideas, and feelings on what it should or shouldn't be—notions that are based on their past experiences and feelings. Sort out yours.

Your Parent ego state contains what you incorporated from your parent figures.	*Yes*	*No*	*Uncertain*
Did your parent figures respect the opposite sex?	____	____	________
Did they seem to respect and enjoy each other?	____	____	________
Do you think their sex life was satisfying to them?	____	____	________
Did they tell you that sex could be joyful?	____	____	________
Do you think their sex life was influenced by their past history?	____	____	________

Your Adult ego state has accurate or inaccurate information.	*Yes*	*No*	*Uncertain*
When dating, was your sexual information sufficient and up-to-date?	____	____	________
Was it sufficient when you got married?	____	____	________
Did you want more information?	____	____	________
Did you get it by personal experience?	____	____	________
From a book?	____	____	________
Did you avoid becoming informed?	____	____	________

Your Child ego state is the child you once were.	*Yes*	*No*	*Uncertain*
Did you play with yourself sexually?	____	____	________

Did you play with others sexually? ____ ____ ________

Were you taught about sex and reproduction? ____ ____ ________

Were you ridiculed for your interest? ____ ____ ________

Were you taught that sex was bad? ____ ____ ________

Were you taught to protect yourself sexually? ____ ____ ________

Did you have disagreeable sexual experiences? ____ ____ ________

Now summarize.

How did your parents, now in your Parent ego state, affect your marriage in the past?

How did the information or lack of information in your Adult ego state affect your marriage?

How did positive and negative sexual experiences in your childhood affect your marriage?

Energy Flow and Personality Structure

Most people have ego state boundaries that are semipermeable. That is, energy can go back and forth from one ego state to another, depending on the situation.

Recall five problems or situations and try to remember quickly and intuitively how you would have responded from each ego state. Try to include words, actions, and feelings. For example, if you had a job you really liked and your marriage partner received a very good job offer that necessitated moving:

Your Parent response

Your Adult response

Your Child response

Which ego state predominated?

Now consider a problem you have actually encountered, such as infidelity, a serious illness, a money disagreement, or simply boredom. How did you respond from each ego state?

My problem ____

My Parent response

My Adult response

My Child response

Which ego state predominated?

Recall other problems you have had. Which ego state in you seems to have been the strongest in the various situations?

Ego States and Views of Marriage

The ego states in any person may agree or disagree about the purpose and nature of marriage. If they agree, a person is likely to conclude, "I'm right." If there is disagreement between the ego states, a person will be less sure and sometimes experience inner conflict.

	Me	*My partner*
P	My parent figures said____ ______________________	Partner's parent figures said ______________________
	They demonstrated their views by______________	They demonstrated their views by______________
A	Information I had about marriage was___________	Information my partner had about marriage was______
	Information I lacked was__ ______________________	Information my partner lacked was___________
C	How I learned or was taught to feel about marriage was ______________________	How my partner learned or was taught to feel about__ ______________________
	How I felt at a deeper level was ________________ ______________________	How my partner might have felt at a deeper level was__ ______________________

Consider how each of your ego states might view marriage. Then fill in the spaces for your marriage partner as well.

If you and your partner have had conflicting views of marriage, which ego state predominated in each of you? Did you work out a compromise or did one of you win and the other lose? How has that affected your marriage?

TA script theory and life plans

According to Eric Berne everyone has a psychological script, similar to a theatrical script. A psychological script can be briefly described as a life plan, very much like a dramatic stage production, that an individual feels compelled to act out. People tend to live by their scripts without realizing that they do so.

Berne said a person in a script is like someone at a player piano, acting as though he or she created the music. Sometimes the person rises to take a bow or a boo from friends and relatives who also believe they are hearing the "player" perform his or her own tune.

Scripts are preplanned productions for the dramas of life. They dictate where people go with their lives and how they are going to get there. Scripts are played out on various "stages," such as home and work. Some people act out the same script wherever they are. Others change scripts when they change stages. They "act" one way at home and another way at work.[3]

The ways people act are often determined by their culture. The culture "directs" the drama and says, in effect, "This is the way it's supposed to be." Consequently, people of a specific race, ethnic background, age, sex, and so forth, may be scripted by the culture to make certain kinds of marriages—traditional, romantic, open, and so forth.

Cultural scripts are the accepted and expected dramatic patterns that occur within a society. They are determined by the spoken and unspoken assumptions about people and events that are believed by the majority of people within that group. Cultural scripts prescribe the traditional ways of doing things. They can be as superficial as wedding ceremony rituals or as deep and important as child-rearing practices or religious convictions.

Like theatrical scripts, cultural scripts have themes, characters, expected roles, stage directions, costumes, settings, scenes, and final curtains. Cultural scripts reflect what is thought of as the national character and can differ widely from one culture to another.[4]

There are three kinds of scripts—constructive, destructive, or going nowhere. In a going nowhere script couples feel stuck in a rut, often bored. They don't solve problems well. For every step forward, they take one backward. In a destructive script they injure themselves—physically or psychologically—or each other. In a constructive script couples recognize their strengths and weaknesses and change what needs to be changed.

Scripting for the five views of marriage

The views people take of marriage are scripted through their cultural expectations, family traditions, and childhood experiences, including pressures from other children.

Marriage as *convenience* is the view most widely held throughout history. Mottoes and other sayings frequently used by parents become scripting directives for their children. Who controls the finances in a marriage can be scripted by parents who said things such as: "A home is a man's castle. He controls the purse strings." Behavior that is observed and copied may also become part of a script.

> *One man who came for counseling was afraid of his wife. She drank heavily and would then become so physically abusive that he slept alone in a room with the door locked for safety. His wife's mother had treated her father in the same way. To protect himself, the father had moved a bed into the garage. The script, from mother to daughter, was to be abusive toward men. In counseling he became aware of his wife's destructive script and his need to get out of it so he would not be a "convenience" to her.*

On a more positive side, a couple can be scripted to practical day-to-day role expectations—who will empty the garbage, put the children to bed, and so forth. These scripting conveniences often change as the partners change.

Marriage as a *spiritual union* is often scripted by religious parents or a religious institution. Words such as "Marriage is a holy sacrament, not to be entered into lightly" reveal a parental concern for a spiritual marriage.

When children observe their parents going to church together or praying together at home, the concept of God as part of marriage may become part of their script. If the children enjoy what they observe, they may copy it. If they don't like it, they may select a somewhat rebellious script and reject the spiritual point of view.

Marriage as *romance* is widely scripted through fairy tales, adventure stories, and TV shows. Sometimes family folklore does the same. Parents who are themselves very romantic and sentimental become models for their children to emulate.

> *This happened to Sylvia, a lovely, tall brunette who walked as though she expected all heads to turn when she entered the room (and they often did). Her courtship with her attractive older husband had been whirlwind excitement. She was also adored by a number of other men her husband didn't know about. Sylvia explained to a friend that when she was very little, her mother, who had the same name, frequently sang her favorite song, "Who is Sylvia, what is she, that all the swains adore her?" Both Sylvia and her mother acted as if troubadours were still available to worship them.*

Marriage as *companionship* may develop for many reasons. Sometimes parents are observed as being good friends. Sometimes people have favorite companions of the opposite sex when they are little. Sometimes the script comes from a favorite story such as Hansel and Gretel, in which children save themselves without help from anyone else.

A *loving* marriage is most likely to be scripted in a loving home where children observe the give and take of daily chores, the give and take in decision making, the give and take of warmth and affection. A loving matrix provides a family stage where a constructive, happy marriage can be acted out, where the lines, the dialogue, the characters, and the scenery are like sunshine that helps people grow.

Personal Roots and Cultural Scripts

In this exercise you can explore some of the roots of your family tree. Alongside the roots in the sketch write in the names of the various cultures of your ancestors. If you are adopted or were raised in an institution and do not know your past, fill in the culture of your adopted parents or of the institution.

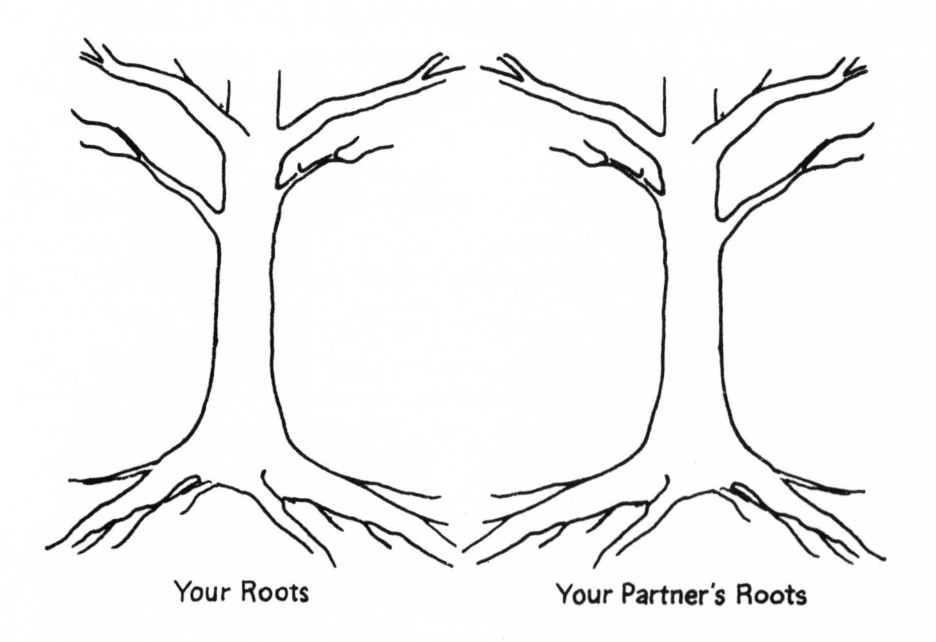

Now consider:

> Do your roots and your partner's roots intermingle anytime in the past?
>
> At what period of time did your roots begin to form a trunk? Use the trunk for your family name.
>
> How would you label the branches?

Cultural Roots and Views of Marriage

Culture can be described in many ways: large or small, exploitive or exploited, warlike or peaceful, free or slave, static or dynamic, religious or not, and so forth. How would you describe your cultural roots? Also, how does your past match up with the past of your partner? You might compare racial, ethnic, and religious backgrounds, as well as other factors.

My ancestral roots	*Words to describe the roots*
______________________	______________________
______________________	______________________
______________________	______________________
______________________	______________________
______________________	______________________

My partner's ancestral roots	*Words to describe the roots*
______________________	______________________
______________________	______________________
______________________	______________________
______________________	______________________
______________________	______________________

> Do you see any patterns or message in your roots that may have affected the past of your marriage?

Subcultural Scripts and Marriage

The deepest roots of your script reach far back in history. Closer to the surface are your roots in subcultures such as a school or religious institutions you attended, a geographical location in which you lived, life-styles of childhood friends, or some other common bond.

Persons in subcultures often identify themselves by using the word "we" and refer to people in other subcultures as "they." Ethnic humor or derogatory terms are other ways of identifying with, or separating oneself from, a specific subculture.

My subculture's effect on our marriage

My partner's subculture's effect on our marriage

How do you *feel* about the above discoveries?

Do you like your roots and your partner's, and their effect on you?

If you have problems in your marriage, are they related to conflicting roots?

When Scripts Are Formed

The experiences children have with their mothers, fathers, and parenting figures are usually the most influential events in the development of a life script. Sometimes parents, like producers of a theatrical drama, initiate some of the positive and negative experiences their children have. Sometimes, like an audience, they respond positively or negatively to experiences their children have with others. Subtle script-reinforcing messages often accompany or underlie parents' words and actions.

List anyone who had a parenting influence on you when you were young, including your mother, father, foster parents, grandparents, or older brothers and sisters. After each name, write something the person said or did that made an impression (for good or ill) on you. Then note what their underlying message was.

Influential people in my childhood	*What they said or did*	*Their underlying message to me*
____________	____________	____________
____________	____________	____________
____________	____________	____________
____________	____________	____________

Drama Stages

Shakespeare's words, "All the world's a stage," provide important insights for your marriage. The home where you grew up was your primary stage. There you learned how to "act"—what roles to play, what dialogue to use, and so forth. Now you still go on stage at times. You may "change the scenery" by redecorating or by cleaning up when company is coming. You may use different "dialogue" when the two of you are alone and when you are with others. All elements of a drama are present in your marriage.

> Imagine that your marriage has taken place on three stages and recall past events that fit the three stages.

Draw stick figures on each stage to represent how you positioned yourselves. For example, was one in the spotlight and the other backstage in a corner? Did you share the spotlight? Take turns?

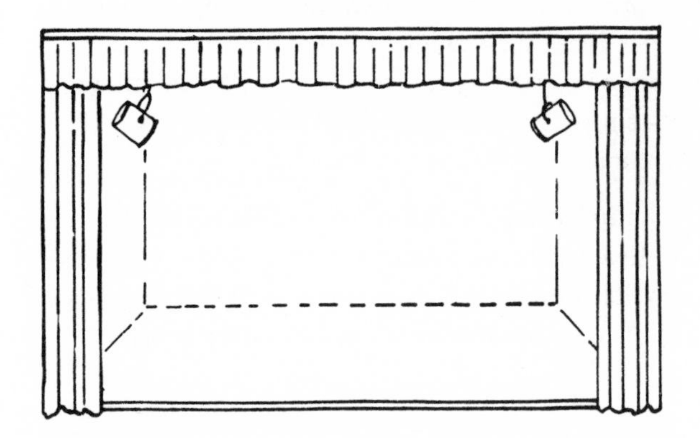

Stage 1

Typical scene when we were alone

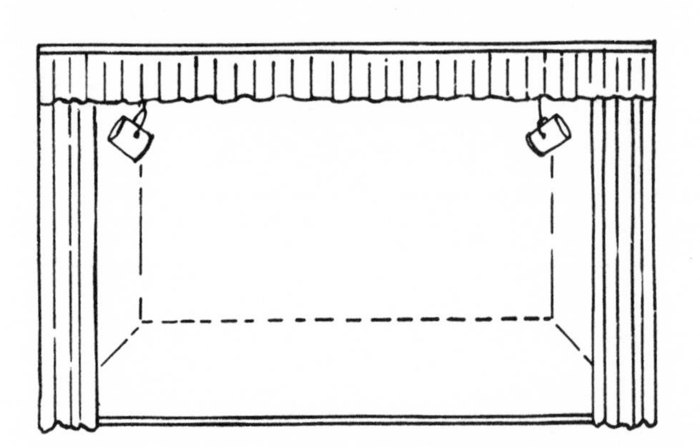

Stage 2

Typical scene when others were around our home

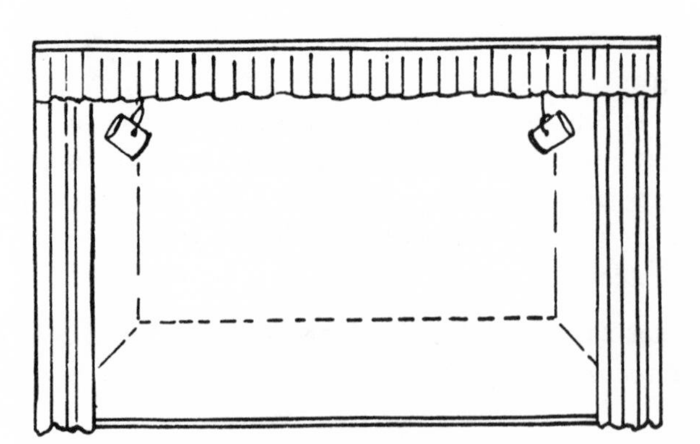

Stage 3

Typical scene when we went out together

Sexual Identity and Scripting Roles

Children are constantly hearing directions from others about how they should live their lives. These messages often have a lasting impact on a child's life script.

Note down some of the messages you remember receiving during childhood concerning the following topics. What was your reaction?

	Message received during childhood	*Its effect on me*
About men in general	____________	____________
About women in general	____________	____________
About being the boy or girl I was	____________	____________
About sexual play	____________	____________
About sex when married	____________	____________
About how to act in other ways when married	____________	____________

Scripting for Male and Female Roles

To get in touch with the scripting messages you received about the division of labor and decision making in a marriage, review the following list. Using the symbol X, indicate who was supposed to do which tasks—according to the messages *you* got when you were little.

	Wife	*Husband*	*Either*	*Both*
Doing dishes	______	________	______	______
Making household repairs	______	________	______	______
Caring for garden	______	________	______	______

Cleaning house	_______	___________	_______	_______
Shopping for groceries	_______	___________	_______	_______
Cooking	_______	___________	_______	_______
Earning money	_______	___________	_______	_______
Spending money	_______	___________	_______	_______
Keeping financial records	_______	___________	_______	_______
Deciding on major purchases	_______	___________	_______	_______
Disciplining children	_______	___________	_______	_______
Nurturing sick children	_______	___________	_______	_______
Playing with children	_______	___________	_______	_______
Planning social events	_______	___________	_______	_______
Making vacation plans	_______	___________	_______	_______

Now, using a check mark, add checks for your *partner's* scripting directions. In what ways are they similar or different?

In the course of your marriage, have you "rewritten" your script in any way by making decisions different from those above?

Drama Roles in Your Marriage

Traditionally, there are three major characters in a drama: (1) the Victim, who appears to be losing but often wins in the end, (2) the Persecutor, who is the "bad guy" and often loses in the end and becomes a Victim, and (3) the Rescuer, who is the "good guy," yet often is victimized by those who really do not want to be rescued.

On life's many stages both partners are able to play the three basic roles. Each may have a "favorite" role, the one that feels most familiar. Each is also able to switch and play the other one's. Victims, for example, while playing a hard role of Poor Me, may actually persecute others with their continuous complaining. Rescuers may overwork their part and end up feeling fatigued or sick—and victimized by others. Persecutors may switch roles and become Rescuers; after yelling angrily, they may apologize and try to make up for it. Of course, people are not always in drama roles. Sometimes they are authentic.

Think of the times when you acted each of the three roles: Persecutor, Rescuer, and Victim. List the ways you felt and acted that fit the role and kept the drama going.

A drama where I played	*Situation where I played the role*	*How I felt*	*What I said and did*
Victim	____________	____________	____________
Rescuer	____________	____________	____________
Persecutor	____________	____________	____________

Type of Marriage Script

This exercise calls first upon your intuition. In the sentences to be completed, fill in the blanks quickly.

What happens to marriages like ours is ________________________

If we go on as we now are, the logical consequences are ________________

____

If our marriage was on stage, would it be like a constructive, destructive, or going nowhere drama? ____________________________

If we wanted to get a better show going, we would need to ____________

______________, instead of ______________ the way we do now.

If an audience was watching us play out our marriage script, the audience

would____

____

If we gave a title to our marriage drama, it could easily be called ___________

____

When I think of that, I feel _______________ and I think _______________

____

If we were to change the drama, we would need to _______________________

____

To do this, we would need to free ourselves from _______________________

____

From past to present

Freedom is not easily won. Throughout history both husbands and wives have been chained to the past in one way or another. Many have not been physically free from the laws, customs, and views of the societies in which they have lived. Even more have not known emotional or intellectual freedom from their own prejudices and inaccurate beliefs.

Today, many traditions of the past are being questioned. Physical freedom is still the basic issue for some. Others struggle toward an intellectual understanding and an emotional maturity to learn from the past while living in the present. Some couples are courageously taking the position that love does not dominate, it motivates.

The motivation pushes them to embark on a journey toward freedom. The journey is not easy—not in the past, not in the present, and probably not in the future. It requires learning how to love and learning how to fight, when necessary, in loving ways. This takes courage—courage to act in spite of feeling afraid. That's what the second part of this book is all about.

The focus of it is on marriage concerns of the present: needs and how they are ignored or met, problems and how (and whether) they are solved, and intimacy in its various forms. The purpose is to show how to combine freedom from the past with courage for the present while striving for a loving marriage.

Part Two

Is the key to love in passion, knowledge, affection?
All three—along with moonlight, roses, groceries,
givings and forgivings, gettings and forgettings,
keepsakes and room rent,
pearls of memory along with ham and eggs.
Can love be locked away and kept hid?
Yes and it gathers dust and mildew
and shrivels itself in shadows
unless it learns the sun can help,
snow, rain, storms can help—
birds in their one-room family nests
shaken by winds cruel and crazy—
they can all help:
lock not away your love nor keep it hid.[1]

—Carl Sandburg

Marriage and the Present

Chapter 5

"I'm afraid to tell you."

"But I want you to tell me the truth."

"If I tell you the truth, you might not like it."

"So what if I don't?"

"If you don't like it, you might leave."

"Well, what *do* you want me to do?"

"I want you to listen."

"I will, I will."

"And just don't say anything."

"Wow, you sure want a lot."

"You're right. I do want a lot. I really need a lot from you."

Sound familiar? The fear to express needs openly *in the present* is a fear many people share. They fear that something catastrophic might happen. They fear a diminishing of self-image or a loss of esteem in the eyes of others. Quite simply, they fear that a need, if verbalized, will not be acceptable to a spouse. Such fears prevent partners from experiencing the deeper love and intimacy that accompanies expressing one's own needs openly and responding to those of a spouse.

Many people are reluctant to say, "This is what I need," or to ask, "What do you need?" They hint at their needs or hide them and resort to psychological games. One person might *hint* of a need for privacy by slamming a door, thus giving the message: "I want to be alone." Another might retire behind a book and frown if someone speaks. A need for "something of my own" may lead a person to maintain a secret bank account. In this case, the need remains forever hidden, without even an external hint.

One couple came to me for counseling because their only child, a boy of eleven, was having severe difficulties at school. The boy was a loner at recess, lunch time, and after school. During classes he spent more time looking out the window than at his books. He seemed to lack energy and his grades were low, although his intelligence was high. At home he was secretive, often withdrawing to his room for hours.

Until his grades indicated that something was wrong, this behavior did not seem strange to his parents. His mother frequently withdrew into daydreaming herself and failed to notice that her son had the same pattern. His father was also secretive, hiding porno magazines behind his workshop tools. The son had copied his father's behavior as well as that of his mother.

In counseling, all three of them talked about the need to be alone, to have more privacy. *Privacy is a basic need.* This family did not recognize, however, that their *real* need was for emotional intimacy and that what they called privacy was really withdrawal based on anger and frustration.

In time, and with help, they were able to develop an atmosphere where, instead of *hinting* at their needs or *hiding* their needs, they could talk about them. Eventually, they discovered healthy ways of meeting their own needs and the needs of each other.

This chapter is about basic human needs and how to recognize them *now*, in the present. Order and security, freedom, risk and courage, property and privacy, respect, trust, equality and truth, commitment and responsibility—all rather old-fashioned words, perhaps, but they speak of basic needs. Some people might think these notions out-of-date or dead in a world that seems so oriented toward acquiring money, possessions, or some other form of power. I hope that's not true for you. I hope these words and concepts can come alive in new ways for anyone who wants a loving marriage.

Present needs and past experiences

The needs that people experience in the present, such as a need for security, are often related to the past. When basic needs are not met in childhood, they may actively surface in the present of a marriage, sometimes in an extreme form. Everyone has the need for physical security, and the terror some people feel when it doesn't exist is very real.

> *Suzanne came for help because, as she explained, "I'm always feeling scared, even when I know there is nothing to be afraid of." Asked when she first started feeling this way, she related how her father used to become very angry at her brother when his grades in high-school Latin were poor. Suzanne, who was four years younger, felt paralyzed when she heard her brother scream as their father beat him in the garage. She thought her father was irrational and was afraid she would be the next victim of his anger. In the struggle to avoid that fate, she tried to get perfect grades, be perfectly polite, and be a perfect daughter.*
>
> *The fear of irrational anger stayed with Suzanne for many years. She felt unable to be assertive if a store clerk even looked irritable. As a teacher, she collapsed into tears when fighting occurred between the seven-year-old children she taught. Unaware of what she was doing, Suzanne married someone who "for no reason" would yell and slam doors—just as her father had. She acted as the proverbial doormat, as her mother had. Until Suzanne suffered severe arthritis, made worse by her internalized, yet unrecognized, anger, it did not occur to her that her own needs had some validity and that as a person she had value. She had to learn how to express her own anger. It was a long hard struggle for Suzanne to grow from feeling fearful and inadequate to feeling courageous and competent.*

I invite you to become aware of your needs more rapidly than Suzanne did. Don't wait for a crisis or some form of psychosomatic illness. Get going. The past does not need to spoil the present.

The importance of order

The concept of order is reflected all around us, in every phase of our existence. Order refers to sequence or arrangement. Summer follows spring; night follows day; the moon has its cycle. People depend on such happenings. They see the universe as essentially orderly. People also depend on the order within their own bodies and within their own lives. They expect their hearts to beat, their brains to function, their stomachs to digest food, their muscles to work in predictable ways.

In addition, people depend on the order provided by federal, state, business, educational, and community organizations. They expect promised pensions to be paid, expect law and order to be upheld, expect essential goods and services to be available, and expect educational opportunities to be provided. Order and predictability are essential needs and are part of all civilized life. Without order, chaos would reign. Whether in nature, our bodies, or our social systems, order provides security and continuity.

Predictable order is an essential need in any marriage, regardless of which view of marriage a person holds. Sometimes daily order refers to orderliness or neatness, as in, "Can't you ever establish some order in this kitchen?" Sometimes it refers to taking orders or giving orders, as in, "Why? Because I said so. That's an order."

The need for order is noticeable in discussions about who's going to do what. Usually, some chores are considered one person's responsibility, while certain others are assigned, either formally or informally, to the other partner. Traditionally, husbands have been expected to perform the financial tasks; women, the household tasks. Although expectancies differ in marriages and although some radical changes are now taking place in role assignments, an orderly "arrangement" of some sort is valued for the predictability, stability, and convenience it affords. In fact, people often select marriages of convenience because of the order they provide—financial, social, family, and sexual.

Orderliness in marriage is often expressed through agreements, sometimes unspoken, regarding how each person will respond to emotional needs—their own or their partner's. For example, if one partner is often tired and emotionally exhausted, he or she may expect the other to be supportive. If one person craves approval, he or she probably has expectations that the approval will be given or withheld. *Many couples are not aware of having made these kinds of agreements.*

Problems can arise in any marriage when people, events, or situations become totally predictable, when everything is too orderly. "Pick up your clothes"; "Don't forget the toothpaste cap"; "Wash your dishes when you finish" are all instructions to be orderly. Order can ruin marriage if it becomes a preoccupation. When there is no planned or random change, no moments of disorder or spontaneity, boredom and resentment are likely to set in. Marriage may begin to be oppressive, and home may feel like a jail with one's spouse as the inflexible jailer.

On the other hand, problems also arise when one partner begins to change and the other doesn't. If a neat person becomes slovenly, if a compliant person becomes assertive, if a sexy person becomes disinterested, if a decision maker suddenly refuses to make decisions, that person is rejecting the "expected" order in a marriage. He or she may have altered certain perceptions or changed priorities, or may be moving toward an altogether new and different order.

Any transition may be slow or rapid. Either speed has its own strains and moments of disorder; yet order is such a crucial human need that people are willing to go through enormous struggles to achieve it.

Any change in order creates stress. Between the times when the old order is experienced and new order is established, people often feel insecure. If the new order, like a company transfer to a new city, is expected to be a *negative* threat to marriage, feelings of fear or hostility are likely to accompany the transition. If the new order, such as a desired pregnancy or big salary raise, is expected to be a *positive* change, feelings of anticipation and excitement are likely.

Maintaining a sense of balance when chaos erupts, or even when things seem slightly out of order, generates anxiety in some marriages. The anxiety can create stress, the stress can lead to illness, and the illness to chaos or to a reordering of important priorities.

Sylvia was overly compliant. She had grown up interpreting the phrase, "Man's home is his castle," to mean husbands should make all decisions and wives should obey them. She deferred to her husband's every whim, almost always prepared the foods he wanted, dressed as he wanted, agreed with his opinions, performed sexually according to his demands. Sylvia did not see herself as an individual with personal rights until an accident incapacitated her for several months. During convalescence, she

> *became aware of how she was undermining the marriage when her husband exploded with, "I'm sick and tired of your acting like a cringing, hurt puppy. I wish you'd get up,* get going on your own, *and get off my back."*
>
> *The confrontation was hard on Sylvia, yet it changed the order in their marriage. She subsequently went to work and developed a new sense of self-esteem. This, of course, did not happen overnight. Her habits of compliance were hard to give up and her husband's habits of dominance were also hard to change. The transition to a new order in their marriage was gradual.*

The need for security

The need for security, which is closely related to the need for order, is both valid and essential. Many marriages, as well as many people, can survive and often grow in times of crisis. When the sense of insecurity continues year after year, however, the relationship itself is likely to break down. Those in the relationship may also experience some kind of personal breakdown—of body, mind, or spirit.

The most devastating threat to a person's sense of security is the feeling of terror that accompanies fear for one's personal safety. Jennifer, a competent computer programmer, described her feelings of intense fear:

> *For years after being raped I felt terror and insecurity. It was early evening. I was going home after work. I lived alone in a small cottage. As I entered my house two men jumped me from behind the door, they had gained entrance through a window. Robbed, beaten, raped, left semiconscious in a city where I felt like a stranger, it was years before I could go to sleep easily. Sometimes I would put a baseball bat under the bed, a whistle, or a knife. At the same time I would worry about whether or not I would be able to even move if someone came in. My fantasy was that I might be too frightened to scream or move. Rage or violence still activates a huge sense of insecurity in me, or if a man I don't know suddenly makes a move toward me I get scared, or when I get home before my husband I'm sometimes afraid to go in the house. Night after night I double-check locks on the doors and windows. I used to sleep with my windows open, because I like fresh air, but I still feel terror when I try to do it. I guess my husband must love me. He doesn't argue about the window, he just holds me quietly when sometimes I cry.*

Other outside threats to security can sometimes be equally devastating: an income too low for basic necessities, unemployment, a terminal illness, a severe accident, or a natural disaster like a flood or hurricane. The stress and anxiety of such experiences may bring a couple closer together, as they develop a team spirit and fight for each other and for their marriage in new ways. By learning to cope, in spite of danger or anxiety, they find their marriage increasingly intimate and meaningful.

Sometimes the threat to security comes from inside the marriage itself. Wife beating is not uncommon, and threats such as, "I'll beat your block off if you . . ." strike fear in the hearts of many women. Some of them retaliate or try to. In recent years, husbands who are battered by their wives are also coming forward to tell their stories. Alice was an angry wife and one who drove irrationally when drunk. When she was in "one of those moods," Sam, her husband, would close himself into the garage for protection against the car she would threaten to run him down with.

Other, more subtle threats become the quiet terrors in many marriages. Flirting with others is one kind of threat; coming home late from work is another. A slammed door, a shrug of the shoulders, disdainful looks, sarcastic remarks, disinterest in the other person's activities are all messages to a spouse that the marriage is in trouble. These messages often add up to, "I might leave you."

Any continuing threat—however minor—will usually destroy romance, companionship, and feelings of love. Yet persons who feel insecure may stay married for a variety of reasons: out of a sense of duty, because the relationship at least provides security of a sort, because they don't want to go through the pain and expense of a divorce, or, in the case of domestic violence, because they fear for their own safety. Although these persons may stay married, they may withdraw emotionally and become frigid or impotent, silent or indifferent.

Freedom in an unfree world

The third basic need in any healthy marriage is freedom—physical freedom and freedom of opinion.

In many cultures, women, whether slaves or ostensibly free individuals, have been denied physical freedom. They have been isolated in the house: upper-class Athenian women in ancient Greece were restricted to their homes; Chinese women, their feet tightly bound, were restricted to the compound.

Although being locked in by a spouse is rare today, many people, men as well as women, do not experience freedom in their marriages. Instead of bolted doors and bound feet, spouses use other means of preventing their mates from interacting with other people: cutting off spending money or leaving a spouse without transportation can be just as effective in some situations. In addition, strong psychological pressures are sometimes used. Social mores may be quoted. Threats of abandonment or physical injury may be made. These psychological forms of harassment are often effective controllers of physical freedom.

"I wouldn't dare leave the house without telling him where I was going," said an attractive college-educated woman. "I'm afraid he'd be furious and start yelling again." "Me go out for a night with the boys?" exclaimed a hen-pecked husband. "If I did that, she'd be cold to me for weeks!"

Many couples argue for hours about freedom and the restrictions they place on one another. "Thelma, it doesn't make any sense for you to get a job," argued Tom, her husband. "I make enough money to support our family and I don't want you out in the business world or joining all those women's liberation groups. I want you home and I think that's where you're supposed to be."

"Well," she retorted, "You go out with the boys and play golf and stuff. Why can't I do what I want to do?"

Attempts to control the movements of one's mate often signal deep insecurity in the controlling partner, as well as in the one who gives in to the controller. It takes courage to break habits like this, yet recognizing the need to do so and the need to be free is an essential first step toward establishing a healthier, more loving relationship.

Eric Hoffer maintains:

> *The real "haves" are they who can acquire freedom, self-confidence and even riches without depriving others of them. They acquire all of these by developing and applying their potentialities. On the other hand, the real "have nots" are they who cannot have aught except by depriving others of it. They can feel free only by diminishing the freedom of others, self-confident by spreading fear and dependence among others, and rich by making others poor.*[1]

Equally important as physical freedom in a marriage is freedom of opinion. This, too, is a basic need. Some couples have an extreme fear of conflict. They confuse agreement with love and believe that disagreement or disapproval will weaken what they perceive as a fragile relationship.

Differences of opinion can be exciting and interesting. They can transform a humdrum relationship into a stimulating one. Politics, property rights, male and female roles, how to rear children, how to spend money, or how to have fun are just a few of the many subjects that couples, living in the present, can choose to discuss—*and differ about.* When both partners in a relationship feel free to express opinions, when they are able to listen intently to each other and respond with respect and candor, new insights are bound to develop.

Some people are unable to distinguish between having an opinion and being right. They fight loudly for their beliefs and may become even more opinionated and stubborn in the process. In effect, they are saying, "I've made up my mind . . . don't confuse me with the facts." These people are not free.

In the past, my husband and I often disagreed on political issues, each of us sure we were right and the other person wrong. Our convictions were so strong that they could have caused a major rift in our marriage if we hadn't eventually agreed that neither one of us could ever know all of the facts, that even TV and the newspapers revealed only some of the truth. Laughingly he said I was incredibly naive (and I sometimes am) and I said he was incredibly prejudiced (and he sometimes is). Prejudice leads to intolerance and interferes with the need for freedom. And intolerance often leads to rigidity.

Why do some people have such rigid beliefs? Generally it is because they have not separated their sense of "this is me" from "this is what I believe." People are more than what they believe. They need to recognize this to achieve personal intellectual freedom and, perhaps more importantly in a marriage, so that they do not try to imprison others by propagandizing, imposing their opinions, and insisting on agreement.

Feelings are often linked to opinions. Feelings, as well as opinions, need to be given free rein. In some marriages only certain feelings are tolerated; others are denied or criticized. One person may loudly and easily express anger. The other may tearfully express inadequacy. Each may tolerate his or her own feeling, yet be intolerant of the other person's: "I can't stand it when you . . . like that." Each partner wants freedom, yet neither partner is willing to grant "equal time" to the needs of their mate.

Risk and the courage to be

Change is frightening to many people. "The old familiar ways may not be good," they say to themselves, "but at least I know where I stand."

Change involves risk and risk implies the possibility of failure. And the possibility of failure requires courage. Yet without some change, without some freshness and newness, marriages often become boring. The partners may *do* many things, but they don't *become* who they could be.

Boredom leads to indifference and physical or emotional withdrawal. Sometimes it leads to anger and violence. Usually it deadens romance and decreases sexual desire. Often it encourages spouses to seek extramarital affairs. Sometimes it motivates them to take a courageous stand, to risk new ways.

When someone who is habitually passive becomes assertive, that may be risking. When someone who is habitually a workaholic becomes more interested in relaxing and enjoying, that may be risking. New ways of behaving upset the order of a marriage; they often involve risk because other people may be surprised, dismayed, or displeased by the changes. Tim, married five years, explained it this way:

> *I love Judy my wife, but sometimes I like to be with the boys and go fishing and have a beer or two. She gets all upset and makes a federal*

case of it and then the whole day is spoiled for me. I wish she'd get some interests of her own instead of being so possessive, jealous, and dependent.

Courage is going ahead and doing something in spite of fear. The opposite of courage, according to psychologist Rollo May, is apathy. It is doing nothing. It is saying to oneself, "Nothing will ever change, so why try?" or, "I haven't the power to change anything, so I'll just have to put up with it."

Not to risk change is to die—or at least to be half-dead. There is nothing in this universe that is not in a continual process of change—knowingly or unknowingly. The stars change in their courses, the earth rotates on its axis, mountains erode, flowers and trees have their limited life spans. And so do people. From the moment of birth they are aging, in both small and great ways.

Change is inevitable and continuous. Partners who are able to accept this fact can take charge over some aspects of their lives. Taking charge is a risk, of course, because a gamble is involved. But not to risk is to avoid an essential part of being human. It is to submit to fate, to feel enslaved instead of working for freedom.

Phillip and his wife Judy came for marriage counseling because of continuing dissatisfaction with their sex life and impending separation. According to him, "She never tries to turn me on. She just lies there and always wants me to take all of the initiative." According to her, "He's always too busy or too tired. When I do make approaches he acts like he just wants to get it over with as quickly as possible. I'm not like that. I'm slower. Yet if I even snuggle up to him for warmth, he's right there right now and it's over in a couple of minutes and I'm left high, feeling sexy when he's gone to sleep. It's agony and I just can't risk it anymore."

The need to *risk* and the courage *to be* are expressed sexually when new techniques are tried, when long-hidden fears and resentments are openly discussed, and when desires and dreams are revealed. For some people, it takes courage to say, "I'm feeling sexy," or, "I want to be close, but I don't want sex tonight," or "I'm going to stop feeling as if I have to perform for you."

Acting courageously is not easy. The courage to *be* as a person is even harder. This kind of courage requires self-valuing of one's inner core just for being, not for performing.

GOOD

Working for freedom is a lifelong task. Martin Luther, writing during the Reformation observed "What else is our whole life on earth than a passing through the Red Sea."[2] Luther was referring to the escape of the Hebrews from their many years of enslavement by the Egyptians. Under the leadership of Moses, they crossed the Red Sea. Luther was implying that all of life is a coming out of slavery—slavery imposed by culture, by outmoded mores, by lack of information, by manipulative people, or by any number of restrictive encounters.

It is not easy to be free. As expressed in the book *Born to Win:*

> *It takes courage to experience the freedom that comes with autonomy, courage to accept intimacy and directly encounter other persons, courage to take a stand in an unpopular cause, courage to choose authenticity over approval and to choose it again and again, courage to accept the responsibility for your own choices, and, indeed, courage to be the very unique person you really are. New ways are often uncertain ways and, as Robert Frost expressed it, "courage is the human virtue that counts most—courage to act on limited knowledge and insufficient evidence. That's all any of us have."*[3]

The need for property and privacy

In a healthy marriage, the need for property and privacy is accepted and respected. Although many couples jointly own property, such as real estate, furnishings, or art, it is important to recognize each individual's need to have "my own things." This may mean a box of tools, a special book of poetry, or a window-box garden. Sometimes these simple material possessions have very special significance, because they are connected with strong memories or experiences.

I often let my old clothes accumulate. I delay throwing them out, rationalizing my inaction by telling myself that they may eventually come back in style. Undoubtedly the real reason I hang on to these clothes is that I can clearly remember a time when, as a young mother, the only clothes I had came from secondhand stores run by the Salvation Army or some other charitable organization.

Occasionally my husband forgets this "hanging on" problem of mine and discards my clothes in what I feel is a premature act. I know he means well, yet I feel betrayed. My privacy has been invaded and my property has been appropriated, and I don't like it. I'm glad it happens only on very rare occasions.

Sometimes the understanding about property and ownership needs to be discussed and perhaps even formalized. Joint property is not necessarily "public property" to be loaned, given away, or thrown away without mutual consent. The most obvious example here is money. Both spouses, whether working or not, need to have some money that they can claim as their own and use as they choose. Still, each needs to be aware of the other's attitude toward money.

My husband and I had a prenuptial agreement that said in essence, "Your money, bills, and children are yours, and mine are mine and neither of us will interfere unless asked." The money part was legalized; the children part was verbalized. With those issues resolved, there was not much left to argue about except, occasionally, politics!

> *Doris and Jack were separating. As a physician, he earned a good income which, according to him, Doris "sure enjoys spending." Though they had been married many years, Jack claimed to still love her intensely. Yet he lamented, "I can't go on anymore. I keep covering for her. She won't stay on any kind of budget. I'm working harder and harder to make more and more money to buy her a fancier house, fancier clothers, a fancier car. I'm really bone tired and just can't go on anymore. Everything we have is in both our names, but she spends so much I haven't a cent for myself and am getting deeper and deeper in debt."*

Marriages like this, in which one partner does most of the giving and the other does most of the getting, are unhealthy.

The need for personal possessions is closely related to the need for privacy. Sometimes this means not opening each other's mail, listening in on each other's phone conversations, or looking in each other's pockets or wallets. More often it means "having my own space."

Part of my privacy is my yellow room. It's where I do most of my writing, and I have planned everything in it just for me—the light yellow carpet and curtains, the flowered drapes, the lime and yellow couch, the light-colored woods of the desk and bookcases. It is not perfect, but it is mine and not to be tampered with. My husband, too, has his own space, a place that bears the stamp of his personality, where his things are arranged exactly as he wants.

Couples also need to realize that each partner needs psychological space, the privacy of dreams, ambitions, and fantasies. It is destructive to a marriage if, when one partner has a fresh idea and enthusiastically shares it, the other responds with a critical, "That will never work. What a dumb plan! What made you think of that!" Some of the best advice I ever heard was, "Respect each other's privacy and deal gently with each other's dreams."

The need for honor, equality, and truth

To respect each other's privacy is not only to respect the privacy of someone's material possessions, it is to respect their personhood—body, mind, and spirit. This honors the *whole person.*

Each of us vitally needs to be honored just for *being a person,* not simply for doing a job. Each of us also needs to be honored for the *tasks* we do, even if these tasks are without fame or fortune, pay or prestige.

Some categories of work are not really honored, not respected by those who do them or by others. Cleaning bathrooms, washing dishes, sweeping the garage, and shoveling snow are all necessary. They lend order to a situation. Yet because of their routineness, because they can be done automatically and without much thought, these tasks carry a low status. Those who do them and those who profit from them may think the work of hands is not as important as the work of the mind. This attitude is mere intellectual snobbery.

When persons or the tasks they do are not honored for their essential contributions to the functioning of a relationship, a false hierarchy of values may be established: "My job is more important than your job." The implication, though seldom verbalized, is: "Because my job is more important, it stands to reason that *I* am more important than *you*." When one person is regarded as more important than the other in a marriage, perhaps because he or she makes more money, feelings of superiority and inferiority are usually present.

Some couples accept these feelings. Their relationships are orderly and predictable. They are not courageous enough to risk what they have for something they may not get—namely, equality of honor. Other couples recognize the need for truth as an essential need of existence, so they are willing to risk.

> *Joy and Herb lived in a small town where most everyone conformed to stereotyped sexual roles: women were mothers and homemakers, men were breadwinners, and each had rigidly prescribed obligations both within the family and within the community. But Joy and Herb were willing to risk disapproval, even avoidance, of friends and sometimes family. Each held a job and they shared household chores equally: cooking, cleaning, child care. They believed themselves to be equally responsible for their marriage and their home, and their actions demonstrated their commitment to equality. When Herb bowed out of the weekly men's club smoker because Thursday was his night to babysit while Joy worked late, the other men in the group thought him henpecked. Even Joy's own mother thought the sacrifice should have been her daughter's, certainly not Herb's. Child care, after all, is a "mother's responsibility."*

Speaking or living the truth is not the same as telling all. It is not a game of "true confessions." Persons who believe in truth speak up or act on their own behalf when the need arises. They risk disapproval from each other. "I can't live with my dishonesty any more," said Greg to his wife. "I've been dating this new woman in our department for two months now. She's sexy and I like it. You've let yourself go. You've gotten fat and careless. I don't want to leave you and the kids, but I can't stand it the way things are around the house."

When a couple decides to live the truth of their marriage, they talk about their basic attitudes and expectations. They struggle together to new levels of understanding. They evaluate the power and conveniences of their marriage, the inclusion or exclusion of the spiritual dimension, the hope for recurring moments of romance to rekindle the fires of passion, the longing for companionship and the need to be friends, and their commitment to love and strive for truth.

Commitment and responsibility

Commitment is a promise or pledge to do something. It involves pledging one's time, energy, body, skills, or possessions to someone else. It can involve a legal contract, as marriage does, or an emotional or intellectual contract. It may occur before marriage or during the process of marriage, with or without the full awareness of those involved.

Living with someone of the opposite sex is not the same as being married. It is neither better nor worse, it is simply different. In spite of the high divorce rate, when people marry they *intend* a long-term commitment. In contrast, many couples who live together seem to commit themselves just for the present, with fewer strings attached. Some stay together as long as their relationship is emotionally, sexually, and economically convenient. But others realize that they want a deeper commitment.

> *Lilly and Steve, a young college couple, had been living together for four years. Undergraduate and graduate school took much of their time, energy, and money—they scraped by financially with part-time jobs and scholarships. When Lilly became pregnant, their relationship became more precious to them. "We want to be good parents," they agreed, "so we want to get married. Most of our friends have been married and divorced. We don't want that to happen and we're willing to work hard on finding out what it means to be really committed to each other. Maybe someday we'll even celebrate our silver anniversary."*

Lilly and Steve did not want the emotional upheaval that comes from one torrid romance after another. They had become close friends. Although it was convenient in many ways for them to live together, with the legal freedom to walk away from the relationship if they wanted to, in marriage they discovered a different kind of commitment, a commitment to each other and to the marriage itself. Because of their commitment, they were willing to accept new responsibilities.

According to the dictionary, to be responsible is to be "legally or ethically accountable for the care or welfare of another." It implies trustworthy performance of a duty or obligation.

Financial responsibility has most frequently been assigned to husbands; caring for a home and rearing children to wives. Both expectations are being modified in many marriages today, where the partners value equality and shun stereotypical sexual roles.

In many previous cultures, intercourse was viewed as a responsibility, and husbands and wives were both held legally responsible for meeting each other's sexual needs, at least on a minimal basis. A six-month period of impotency or a refusal to engage in sexual activities was often grounds for divorce—even in societies that did not easily sanction divorce.

Ethical accountability, as well as legal responsibility, has also fluctuated greatly. What is accepted as permissible in some societies is thought immoral in others and may be punishable by death. Since the beginning of civilization, adultery has often been a capital crime. No longer. Today, some couples take it for granted. Michael, a thirty-year-old traveling executive, stated his position this way: "Why not? Louise isn't interested in sex, so I get it from other women." Louise's only response was, "Don't tell me about it and don't get it here in this town where other people might find out."

The term *situational ethics* was coined to explain that what is permissible in one situation may not be in another. According to Erik Erikson:

> *It is clear that he who knows what is legal or illegal and what is moral or immoral has not necessarily learned thereby what is ethical. Highly moralistic people can do unethical things, while an ethical man's involvement an immoral doings becomes by inner necessity an occasion for tragedy.*[4]

The ethical implications that go along with responsibility often create inner turmoil when values are in conflict. Such was the case with Nancy, seventeen-years-old and seven months pregnant, who was arrested for shoplifting infants' clothes. "I couldn't help it," she sobbed. "Randy doesn't want the baby, so he won't give me any money to buy anything. What can I do!"

All relationships have implied responsibilities. Responsibilities may be met willingly or resentfully, or avoided altogether. Sometimes responsibilities are not met because they are not discussed. One partner may operate on the "crystal ball" theory—in other words, he or she assumes the other "knows" what is wanted. "He knows that I need him," she may say to herself. And he may be saying the same words silently.

The need to be needed is strong. Yet people often become overcommitted and shrink from the burden of further responsibility. A person who is overly dutiful or in a state of continual compliance to others may suddenly revolt and insist on freedom. "I want to be free to be me," or, "I want to do what I want to do," are statements commonly expressed by people who have taken too much responsibility for others and not enough for themselves.

We all need to take more responsibility for ourselves. An hour a day, just for oneself, is a place to start. I often enjoy the hour just before and as the sun comes up. For me it is a meditative time. There is a different kind of stillness and movement at that early hour. The air smells and feels silky on my skin. I like to look out the window and see the wind rustle a tree or a covey of quail strut across the lawn. Geronimo, our one rooster, crowing to waken his harem of ten hens, welcomes the day. I feel it is my hour to experience myself as part of the universe, to become aware of my senses again after a night of sleep, to think and plan if I want to, to nonthink and nonplan if that is my choice for the moment. This hour is part of my responsibility to myself. I am committed to it. As a result, I am more useful to myself and to others during the day that follows.

Everyone wants to feel useful. Yet many people come to identify themselves soley with their responsibilities. When these responsibilities end—when retirement comes or the children leave home—such people feel useless and empty. They have not developed enough personal interests in earlier years. Because of their age or infirmities, they may not have as much energy as they once did. Therefore, they may not feel motivated to assume a new commitment to themselves individually or to reaffirm their commitment to each other. In a youth-oriented culture such as ours, it takes courage to invite a spouse to grow old in a loving marriage, as did the poet Robert Browning:

> *Grow old along with me!*
> *The best is yet to be,*
> *The last of life, for which the first was made.*[5]

Couples who want to create more loving marriages need to "own up" to who they are—as individuals and as a couple. This will permit them to enjoy the commitment and stop dreading some of the responsibilities. They can create situations that call for new efforts. They can give each other the opportunity to make joint decisions. They can see how a particular task fits into a larger pattern. When this happens, a deeper sense of trust is experienced.

Trust and forgiveness

When a marriage is entered into as "holy matrimony," vows to "love, honor, and cherish" are often taken. To some people these words are sacred vows that reflect a spiritual relationship. One woman came for counseling because her husband wanted a divorce. Between sobs she blurted out, "We both believed our marriage was made in heaven. We were even baptized together and it was very, very special. How could this happen? If it was made in heaven, how could it go down the drain?"

To other people the words "holy matrimony" reflect an archaic social ritual. When marriage is a social ritual, it is based on some form of convenience. The trust level of each person for the other is based on *doing,* not on *being.* For example, one might say, "I trust you to keep the house in order," or, "I trust you will be nice to my friends," or, "I trust you to watch our budget carefully." When used in this way, trust is an expectancy that a person will perform in specific ways.

In a marriage that is experienced as a sacred relationship, the sense of trusting someone acquires a spiritual dimension. The partners rely on each other's integrity. They firmly believe that their mates can be counted on, not just for what they do, like honoring commitments and taking responsibility, but for who they are in the very essence of their being. To be trusted in this way is to be honored.

The loss of trust is devastating, and unfortunately, many couples experience this agony. "But I trusted you and you let me down," is a common lament. Confession, restitution, and forgiveness are necessary in any marriage of couples who believe in truth. Sometimes the process is more crucial than at other times. No one is perfect. Everyone gets hurt and hurts others, however good his or her intentions are.

Infidelity is often the most painful cause of marital collapse. When it happens, the partner who is let down may feel abandoned, betrayed, and unable to forgive. The person who is unfaithful may justify his or her actions in some way, yet the intimacy bond of trust is damaged, sometimes irreparably.

> *"It didn't mean anything to me," said Fred defensively. "It was just like a one-night stand. You were working late, and your friend Edith came over. We were just sitting there having a couple of drinks and both feeling lonely, so we ended up in bed. But it didn't* mean *anything."*
>
> *"Maybe not to you," sobbed Peggy, "But I lose my husband and my best friend, both on the same night. Can't you see what this means to me? I'll never be able to feel trust for either one of you again and I just can't stand it. I hurt so much."*

Losing trust in oneself is also devastating and many individuals experience this personal despair. Surprisingly, "I can't trust myself," is as common as, "I can't trust you." Losing trust in oneself occurs in many ways: People do not live up to their values, or they give in to parts of themselves they don't like, or they break their own commitments. One man described the pain of a loss of self-trust:

> *I was so stupid for giving in to temptation. Now I feel so guilty I feel like killing myself. You see, I promised myself and my wife to stay away from bars. I knew I couldn't be around liquor without acting like a thirsty horse. Then I stopped for a few on the way home. Then I rear-ended the car in front, and a child went through the windshield and is all cut up. What's the matter with me? Why don't I keep promises to myself?*

When people don't keep their promises, they often experience a deep sense of guilt, and often a sense of loneliness. In the above case, the man did not forgive himself. He committed suicide. He did not seek the opportunity to try to make restitution and to be forgiven.

To recognize the problem when trust is lost is to begin to face the truth. Sometimes this means owning up to errors and asking for forgiveness. Sometimes it means giving up unrealistic expectations of others and forgiving them for being human. Sometimes it is to look in a mirror and say, "This is who I am, inside as well as outside. It's time to face the truth of myself."

When people own up to something, they stop being defensive, they stop justifying and intellectualizing, and they stop acting as victims and persecutors. They begin the process of forgiving.

The words *forgive* is defined as to "grant pardon without harboring resentment." Thus, forgiving has two parts: granting pardon and giving up resentments.

Pardon is a release from punishment. Punishment may be nonverbal, perhaps indifference to sex, withdrawing from conversation, being late, hiding feelings, and so forth. Or it may be verbal: "I'll never trust you again"; "I'll never feel the same"; "I can forgive but I'll never forget." Sometimes partners punish each other without being fully aware of how much pain they are inflicting. To forgive is to stop saying and doing things merely to punish someone.

Forgiveness involves letting go of self-righteousness and feelings of blamelessness, stopping oneself from saying, "Well, it wasn't my fault. You're the one who did it." That kind of statement is a punishment, not a release. It communicates hate, not love. It reveals resentment, not forgiveness.

It's difficult to give up resentment when there is little or no trust. A deep understanding of how a major problem develops, hours and hours of talking and sharing—feelings as well as thoughts—are often necessary before forgiveness can occur.

No one can be "trusted" to be perfect. Perfection is not a worthy goal; wholeness is. And wholeness is a lifelong task. Life is a pilgrimage, often from one need, one problem, one solution to another. Pillow talk between partners can soften a rocky pilgrimage.

Chapter 6

"You told me you'd come right home."

"Well, I know it, but I just stopped and had a drink with the guys."

"Yes, but the dinner is all cold."

"Well, I don't care, let it go."

"I do care. The children and I have been waiting two hours."

"There you go again . . . nag, nag, nag."

"You never look at things from my point of view."

"I wish I hadn't come home at all."

Problems in Marriage

When needs are not met, when views and values are in conflict, problems emerge. In the desperate striving for romance and emotional or financial security, many couples do not even pause to consider that they will have problems in their marriages. They dream of perfect happiness and don't permit thoughts of a harsher reality to creep in. They do not want to admit, or perhaps never even realize, that problems will continually arise in any marriage and that learning how to recognize and solve them can be an exciting process, one that leads to new understanding of themselves as well as their partners.

Some people actually like problems. They consider them a challenge. They want to be involved in issues that call on their interpersonal skills. They enjoy the evaluation that accompanies changing careers, changing residence, or even buying a car.

Other people avoid problem solving at all costs. They may be short of money and refuse to balance the checkbook. Their children's report cards may indicate trouble in school and they avoid talking to the teachers to try to find out why. They ignore complaints from their spouses about boredom and the use of leisure time.

Yet all of life involves problems and every marriage is going to have both personal and interpersonal ones. The problems may be *minor:* "Where's the toothpaste cap? It's off again." "Isn't it *your* turn to empty the garbage?" "Who's driving the kids to the movies?" Or they may be *major:* "I lost my job today." "My mother is too old to take care of herself. She'll have to live with us." And, unfortunately, some problems are *catastrophic:* "Come to the hospital. The kids have been in a bad auto accident."

Recognizing exactly how serious a problem is helps to put it in perspective. Many people refuse to recognize their problems until it's too late. They deny, avoid, or procrastinate about solving minor problems. So minor problems become major problems, and the major problems may escalate into crisis situations with catastrophic endings. A marriage that could have been saved may be destroyed. Laura told this story:

> *We had been married only six months when Jay said he wanted a divorce to be with someone else. As I look back on it now after many years, my hunch is that he suddenly realized that having two stepchildren was more than he wanted. At the time I thought I had covered all potential problem areas by promising to support myself and my children. But I had overlooked the fact that Jay just wasn't used to kids.*
>
> *I clearly remember that night. It was awful. It literally knocked the wind out of me and I couldn't breathe. The next day, I agreed to see his at-*

> *torney, who was his personal friend. The attorney turned out to be my friend as well. He offered this challenge: "Can you stand it if he goes out a lot nights? Can you stand it and not say anything to precipitate a fight or aggravate him so he will pack up and leave? Can you stand acting sexy and loving in spite of your feelings?"*
>
> *I decided I could if I had to. So I did. Four months later he came home and said, "I was a damn fool. She threatened to kill herself if I didn't leave you for her. Will you take me back?" I replied, "I never really let you go. Come close."*

Laura found a successful, although painful, way to nurse her marriage back to life. But maybe if both of them had been more sensitive to the need for time alone with each other, without the children, perhaps the situation would not have happened.

Sometimes problems are obvious—views or values on politics or how to raise children or how to handle money differ significantly. Many times, however, problems are far more subtle. Couples who are not in the same space or time or who are bored with each other or the marriage can face serious problems and not be aware of their importance.

This chapter shows how to recognize subtle as well as obvious problems, how couples react to problems, and how to develop specific plans to solve problems. Finally, it is about what to do when there is no solution except to let be and to let go.

Needs, views, and value collisions

Problems crop up in marriage when individual needs are not met, when values conflict, or when partners have differing views of marriage and each other.

Needs have to be met if the physical, emotional, and spiritual health of a person are to stay intact. Needs can often be met by an object, like a lock on a door that satisfies a need for physical security. Or, they can be met by an action, like a hug that helps to satisfy a need for emotional security. These objects and actions signify that the need is recognized and being responded to by the other person.

In a needs conflict, the people involved have divergent needs and can usually point to some concrete, tangible effect the need is having on them. For example, partners together on a holiday may experience a needs conflict when one needs sleep and says, "I can't keep going without more rest," while the other needs exercise and says, "I'm uptight if I don't use my muscles."

When caught in a genuine needs conflict, some people are willing to compromise or postpone relieving their needs, since their "relationship" is more important to them than a specific need. Others are not. When compromise is impossible, views or values may be at the heart of the problems.

Views of marriage are attitudes regarding the way things are in a marriage and how they should or shouldn't be—convenient, spiritual, romantic, compassionate, or loving. Problems arise when couples have different basic views of their marriage. If he wants the excitement of romance, but she wants the comfort of companionship, their conflicting views may affect other aspects of their marriage: where they go for vacation, how they relate to their friends, how they spend their money. If she's deeply religious and all he wants is for her to fill the role of a good "company wife," they may have constant conflicts over her religious commitments versus his business activities and ambitions.

Views can be changed or modified in many ways. When one person makes a genuine effort to look at something from the other partner's perspective and to see it through his or her eyes, views are likely to change. Any point of view may change gradually, or may involve a sudden awareness that the reality of marriage takes many forms.

People also hold distinct views of their partners and of the role each should play in the marriage. These views can be compatible or at odds. In some marriages, for example, the partners share certain times when they regard each other closely, both physically and psychologically—during an intimate evening before a roaring fire, across the breakfast table, in bed late at night. They also have periods when they see each other as though from a distance—when they go their separate ways for individual concerns such as work, school, or a hobby.

Sometimes attention may be sharply focused, like a spotlight on a stage, or diffuse, like a floodlight that bathes the entire stage in light. In a marriage, one person may focus on the small details of living—an unmade bed, the disorder of the Sunday paper—while the other may be concerned with maintaining a warm, comfortable atmosphere—a wider perspective.

This spotlight-floodlight way of seeing things is often related to sex roles. Most men traditionally focus on one particular job at a time and spotlight things. Women's traditional role as wife and mother has required dividing attention between several things at once: a crying baby, a boiling pot, a ringing telephone. Any person can see things both ways or can supplement another's point of view.

When these views come into conflict—when one spouse is concentrating on petty annoyances while the other is blind to these day-to-day problems—a couple can experience a serious difficulty without even being able to identify the crux of the problem.

Values are the beliefs people live by, fight for, and sometimes are willing to die for. Many people are not fully aware of their values or the priorities they have assigned to them. Values are fundamental personal beliefs about the meaning and significance of oneself, others, or the world. Important values and beliefs continually influence a person's thoughts, feelings, attitudes, and behavior.

Certain values, such as security, freedom, salvation, justice, unity, friendship, and so forth, are major values. They give a person's life its direction, its character, and its goals.

Other values that directly influence people's daily activity and interaction might be labeled everyday values. These include cleanliness, efficiency, orderliness, helpfulness, creativity, affection, promptness, cooperation, attractiveness, and so on.

As individuals verbalize or act out their values, they tend to reveal who they are. Values help to define personal identity, as a religious person might value salvation or a scientist might value truth. Since values are an essential part of one's self-image, to enter a value collision is to put oneself on the line. A value collision also challenges others' fundamental beliefs about themselves and about "how things should be." Collisions between people often occur when their values are challenged or threatened."[1]

If one partner is practicing something the other considers immoral or unethical, like participating in payoff bribes at work, or using corporal punishment, or being unfaithful, these conflicts become major problems themselves and often tear marriages apart.

Needs, views of marriage, and even values sometimes change as people grow older and as marriages evolve. Sometimes partners can fill each others needs; sometimes they can't. Sometimes they have the same views of marriage and similar values; sometimes they don't. Most of the time these conflicts and problems can be resolved. But, unfortunately, there are instances when the divisions are too great. To decide whether a given conflict is resolvable, it helps to clarify whether only needs are at stake, whether views are inconsistent, or whether personal values are on the line. Many marriage problems may involve all three.

The following example from a marriage counseling session illustrates how the three are related:

Husband: *I'm just not getting enough sex at home. My wife is so cold.*

Wife: *If he would just bring me a flower I'd be interested. I need to know he cares for me. Even a single flower could turn me on.*

Husband: *That's kid stuff—flowers and all that jazz.*

Wife: *Maybe so, but then I feel warm and as if you care for me. Not just like you're using me as some kind of object. When you just use me that way I feel like a garbage can. I feel dirty, not loved.*

Husband: *Well, I'd love you more if you'd entertain my clients more.*

And on and on it went. In the past, this couple's problem was one of conflicting needs: his sexual needs versus her emotional security needs. It was also a conflict of views. To him, marriage had been for sexual and social convenience; to her, it was for romance. Their problems first arose the second year after marriage, when the honeymoon was over and the sexual attraction and romantic infatuation had begun to fade. When dating, they had talked about the possibility of true intimacy—sexual and emotional—but ten years of routineness and ignoring small problems had dampened their hopes. Without freshness, newness, excitement, and openness, their relationship had remained at a surface level instead of growing deeper.

Convenience had become the primary reason for their marriage. Although she had not quite given up the possibility of romance with him, his role as father and breadwinner had become more important. He was focused on getting ahead, on being a financial success on the job, and he wanted her emotional support for this. He especially wanted her to be an entertaining, charming hostess for his clients.

Both had begun to feel more and more strongly about the "rightness" of their own views and the wrongness of the other person's view. The stronger they felt, the more they were polarized. The polarization became a value and their values were in collision.

An angry year of separation was followed by divorce. Three years later, they remarried each other. "We're battle-scarred," they said, "but we're going to *work for our marriage* now, not just for ourselves."

The process from experiencing needs to becoming aware of views of marriage to analyzing how the views are related to the values is:

Physical and emotional needs	Views of marriage	Value beliefs	Resolution or conflict

When values are compatible, problems are usually worked through in some way. When they are not, conflict may erupt, emotional or physical withdrawal may occur, and separation and divorce may follow. Usually this brings anguish to one or both partners. Emily Dickinson said it well:

> *Parting is all we know of heaven,*
> *And all we need of hell.*[2]

Money, children, and in-laws problems

Arguments and misunderstandings about money, in-laws, and children are the stuff of situation comedies and melodramas—and of almost *everyone's* everyday life. Chances are you've experienced at least one of these, and more probably all three. There often seems to be no solution to these frequent hassles—squabbling about the children, the budget, or each other's parents becomes an expected, an accepted routine. Yet these squabbles can often slowly erode a marriage; either their sameness and pettiness become boring, or they escalate into more major crises. Unless daily logistical problems, such as who'll balance the checkbook or change the baby's diapers, are talked about and solved, they can hinder a marriage's growth.

Money mess-ups are so common that many couples expect them to continue for a lifetime—and consciously or unconsciously make sure that they will. Using credit cards indiscriminately, refusing to stick to a firm budget, going on buying sprees, gambling at cards or the race track, overspending for housing, clothing, recreation, furniture, and so forth all easily lead to serious money difficulties. Sometimes one partner acts like an impulsive child, spending with no thought for the future. The other partner may act as a controlling parent ("You know we can't afford that. The last thing we need now is a new television."). This often works for a while—but only for a while.

Prevention is a great plan—to know how much money is coming in, to prepare a budget, and to stick to it. "We do that," a young couple with three children complained, "but we had no idea that Joe was going to be transferred *and* that I'd have to quit my job to go with him *and* that Mary would need braces on her teeth.'' Unexpected events are common in any marriage, and a couple needs to have an emergency fund they can draw on quickly. Refinancing a house or car, or taking out a personal loan are possible ways to get needed cash. However, to do so may precipitate a larger crisis at a later date. Determining a specific amount of money to set aside in a savings account regularly and not drawing on it except in emergencies (even for something ''important,'' like new furniture) is the best way to avoid money problems.

''That seems like such a drag,'' said Joe when this program was suggested by a financial advisor. ''I don't want to go through life just being careful and not having any fun.'' The solution for Joe's boredom is a ''slush'' fund, money that each person can spend without accounting for it to the other. This fund needs to be realistically budgeted along with utilities and other payments. Not to do so could be disastrous for couples like Joe and Mary, for without a planned ''escape hatch,'' their daily routine may become an intolerable grind.

Issues about how to rear children—how to nurture them, discipline them, help them in the many ways children need help—often interfere with a couple's marriage relationship. Like money mess-ups, the problems of being parents may be denied, avoided, argued about, or assigned to one person, with little involvement by the other person. Naturally, this often leads to resentment. The only solution is talking about it and taking action. Children need both of their parents and they need to have them agree, not fight, about most things.

Major problems in families often emerge because of a parent-child power struggle. Sometimes the struggle is open and aboveboard: ''Do what I tell you, young man.'' ''I *don't* want to.'' Pow! Sometimes the power struggle is less obvious, perhaps taking the form of procrastination: ''Do as I tell you, young man.'' ''Yeah, Dad, after the TV show is over. It just started. And then I have to make a couple of phone calls and fix my car a little, but I will. Don't worry.'' Hours later the chores are still not done, and Dad has either worked himself into a rage or hopelessly given up on his requests.

Why do these kinds of struggles often become major sources of dissatisfaction? It involves a difference in values—a clean and tidy house may be an achievement that has meaning for parents, but no meaning for their children. So a simple issue like cleaning one's room may become a major value clash. When that happens, appreciation and acceptance of each other is difficult. A family is a system. If one person is in pain or in trouble, so are the others.

Suzy was brought in for counseling because she was misbehaving in school and picking on her younger sisters, Phyllis and Margaret. The parents regarded Suzy as the problem, while Suzy thought her sisters were the problem. She said, "They gang up on me. Dad always sticks up for them while Mom leaves the room." It turned out that Suzy was Mom's by a previous marriage. Phyllis and Margaret were "theirs" and the father was very partial to his "own" daughters. Mom was afraid that if she stood up for Suzy, he might leave.

Being a stepparent is a tough job. Frequently, the stepparent joins his or her new family with no idea of how extremely difficult it is to enter a family that has been traumatized by death or divorce. No matter what the cause of separation, neither the original bonding between mother and child in the womb nor the early bonding with a father can be undone. When stepparents try to break this bonding, everyone suffers. Everyone also suffers when expectancies are unrealistic or romanticized.

Stepparents and stepchildren should not be expected to love and accept each other just because of the new marriage. Loving takes time; perhaps it may never happen. Insecurity, guilt, and resentment are emotions frequently experienced by every member of the family. Power struggles are very common, especially if the new marriage quickly follows a death or divorce. Children may feel the need to be loyal toward their natural parents and may feel disloyal if they begin to like a stepparent. The stepparent, usually out of jealousy, may subtly or not-so-subtly criticize the natural parent and try to separate the children from their past. It seldom works.

Problem-solving skills are needed—almost every inch of the way. If the family as a whole is important, not just the spouse, a couple will persist, hard as it may be, in acting in lovable ways toward children and stepchildren who themselves may sometimes act in extremely unlovable ways.

Problems with in-laws can be as troublesome as problems with children. Most people feel some defensiveness about their families and some resentment toward the loyalty a spouse feels for his or her own. It's easy to fall into a pattern of criticism: "If you love me, you wouldn't talk that way about my relatives." "Your mother's always criticizing me." "I don't like your father using swear words around our children."

The solution is unbelievably simple: Don't criticize. Sympathize if need be, but don't criticize. People who freely criticize their own families may become immediately belligerent if an "outsider" dares to do the same. In some marriages, a spouse is considered to be more of an outsider than are parents, brothers and sisters, aunts and uncles, and so forth.

Grandparents, parents, in-laws, and other relatives may present problems in families as they get older and are less able to care for themselves. They may need emotional and financial support. In some families, older relatives are loved and respected for their wisdom, their insight, and their sacrifices over the years; in other families, they are tolerated; in still others, they are avoided, ignored, or actively disliked, because of the needs they impose on the family or because their values conflict sharply with those of younger family members.

It has been estimated that one-third of the elderly single people in the United States live with their children. Sometimes it works; sometimes it's disastrous. Often the critical determining factor is how well the parents and grown children got along before this kind of living situation was attempted. If their relationships were harmonious, the chances of success are greater than if they weren't.

Even when parents or other relatives do not live with their married children, problems arise. The parents may be exploited for more money, more babysitting, or more of something else. The children may also be exploited in similar ways. Needs are often in conflict and values often collide. Marriages meant for loving may turn into endurance contests unless problems are recognized and limits are established. Establishing limits is often difficult.

> *Jean, a young, attractive wife and mother, came to counseling complaining about her widowed mother. "I have no time for myself," she moaned, "I have to spend so much time on the phone comforting Mom." Unknowingly, Jean was using her mother as an excuse for not facing some of her own problems. When she decided to set limits and phone her mother every other day instead of twice a day, her marriage began to improve. She also blushingly reported that her mother was looking and feeling better, and had told her, "Jean, I'm glad you're developing a life of your own. I love you, but I didn't want to be on the phone so much and I didn't know how to tell you."*

Problems of crisis

At one time or another, every marriage will be tested by the most obvious of all problems—a crisis. The crisis may be sudden, unexpected, and traumatic, like a car accident, a fire, or a crippling illness. Shock and disbelief are typical responses to such traumas.

Many marriages also have crisis *periods.* These generally lead to an expected conclusion, such as death after a long illness, being fired after trouble at work, getting sued for not paying bills, and so on. Many of these kinds of expected crises are preceded by a waiting period. For example, waiting for the inevitable death of an elderly parent, waiting to see if a child will recover from a serious illness, or waiting to see if a pay raise is forthcoming. Most crisis periods are punctuated by crisis moments. These are often spoken of as the time when "the die is cast" or when "there's no going back."

In some crises, such as a natural catastrophe, people feel as if they have no control over their destinies. In other crises, they know they do have control and that the outcome will depend on the decisions they make. This is often anxiety provoking. Most people want to make the "right" decision, yet, in some instances, they are forced to choose between two equally poor solutions. Thus, what to do when faced with crises becomes important.

Some people respond well to crisis situations. They usually have the reputation of being "people you can count on" because they activate their physical and intellectual skills to meet the problem head on. They know, for example, that recovery often follows illness, that renewal of mind and emotions, as well as renewal of the body, is possible. They know that a built-in drive for health is part of being human. They know that much of life is a do-it-yourself problem-solving process.

Others do not have this knowledge or the confidence it provides. In crises they become helpless and are generally described as "people who fall apart when needed most." Their self-images are likely to suffer as a result. One young mother defined herself thus: "I'm so insecure, I just fall apart at the seams if anything at all happens to the kids. Then I have to phone someone for help and I can hardly dial the number. After the crisis is over I usually feel sick and upset for days."

Catastrophe is more than a crisis. Usually it has tragic dimensions. Yet, it does not have to be the end of life or the end of a marriage.

> *Lenor, one of my step-daughters, age thirty-two, beautiful and talented, caring and deeply committed to her farmer husband and two very young daughters, was riding horseback one day when she discovered a hard lump in her groin. Rapid medical consultations and a biopsy led to amputation at Mayo Clinic of one leg and part of a hip.*
>
> *Seemingly overnight, Lenor became, in most people's eyes, radically handicapped. Not in Lenor's own eyes, however, nor in the eyes of her husband. It was a problem, they agreed, but it did not need to be a*

catastrophe. She was still wife and mother. With sheer determination, Lenor broke herself of the drug addiction that had developed because of the drugs administered to relieve her excruciating pain. With sheer determination, she rejected a wheel-chair and learned to walk with an artificial leg that matched her own, though it had to be strapped around her waist. She learned to swim once more (though this time like a mermaid), and to ride horseback again with a substitute leg designed just for that purpose, and to stay beautiful at the proper weight. And to stay sexy and to learn how to be that way with one leg.

Catastrophe? Not really. She and her husband know that marriage is for loving, and loving always has problems, and problems can be solved.[3]

In and out of space

Just as every marriage will confront *obvious* problems—differing needs, views, and values, as well as occasional crises—every marriage will also face more *subtle* difficulties—problems of space, of time, and of boredom.

Couples sometimes fail to recognize the importance of space—both physical and emotional. They are not aware of what it's like to be in or out of space with each other, except at a superficial level.

Space and place are closely related, but are not the same. The word *place* usually refers to a geographical area. *Space* is more often defined as the intuitive three-dimensional field.

Body space is a popular phrase to indicate the differences some people have in claiming their space. When sleeping, the desired space may be small; when dancing, it may be large. The new vogue of "touch" dancing is a return to the thirties and forties, when couples enjoyed bodily closeness in the same space rather than "doing their own thing" in their own space.

Some people are out of touch with their body space. They may be ashamed, even disgusted, with the way they look, or the way they act, so they become unaware of what is happening inside their body space or how their bodies occupy space in the outside world. It may take an illness or an accident or a crisis of loneliness for them to become aware of their body space and needs.

Sometimes efforts are made to prevent people from this awareness. If in pain, they may be given drugs that result in a feeling of detachment from their bodies. In fact, they may describe the drug experience as an "out-of-body" experience. One injured man said, "There I was outside my own body, looking down at it.'' Another hospitalized man reported, ''I didn't leave my body, all of me just floated off into space.''

Some people claim the same kind of experience when they are asleep and dreaming. They often feel and report that they were really somewhere else. Nevertheless, each person has a *physical* space, a contained area that they feel should not be violated. Sometimes this space is constant—a special room, a getaway hiding place, perhaps just a drawer of personal possessions. A person's space can also be temporary—when Sharon goes to the library on Tuesday evenings she prefers to be alone, without intrusion. She calls the library her ''space.'' The physical space of others, as noted in the last chapter, is a basic need. If it is constantly violated—by one partner who, for example, is ''cleaning up'' the other's desk or woodworking bench—then they inevitably have problems.

Some people need more physical space than others. They may have grown up in a spacious home or in a crowded household where there was little privacy. Such people especially value retreating to their private spaces and may also attach more importance to their personal belongings. Some cultures and families encourage people to ''keep their distance;'' wars are even fought for extra space.

Each person also has an *emotional* space, the privacy of thoughts and dreams. Problems arise when couples seldom share the same emotional space. They may be physically together, but their minds are wandering to other places, other people. Sometimes this happens when a husband or wife constantly ''brings home the office.'' One partner may be talking about money problems or the children and, although the other feigns interest, he or she is really thinking about the profit-and-loss statement for the department. Inevitably, of course, this will happen from time to time, but when it becomes a pattern—when she is always thinking about being somewhere else with another lover, when he is constantly fantasizing about trips to far lands and new financial schemes, then they are not sharing their essential selves with each other. They are not there emotionally; *perhaps* in some sense, not physically!

My husband and I have an agreement: every once in awhile we will ask each other, ''Where are you now?'' and we answer as quickly and as honestly as possible. Some of the replies are amazing! Seemingly we may be driving in the car to Sacramento, but at some other level of existence I'm with my grandchildren swimming and he's on the golf course shooting an almost-par game. That simple question, ''Where are you?'' often brings us back to the same space.

Currently there is great interest in the field of parapsychology in what is called "out-of-body experiences." According to people who have such experiences, or report having them, some part of their essential personalities or spirits leaves their bodies temporarily and then reenters them. In the world of medicine, researchers in death and dying have taken an interest in the out-of-body experiences reported by people who have come close to death or who have actually been declared medically dead and have come back to life.

It is not uncommon for people to comment on "being in two places at once." Fantasies often have the power to "take" us to another place, and a letter may "bring" a faraway person back.

In a loving marriage, a couple need not always *be* physically close in order to feel one another's presence. When they are separated because of work, illness, the demands of other people, and so forth, they may still *feel close* to each other.

I recently observed a romantically attached lover, separated from his love, sitting on a porch with a group of people. Several in the group spoke to him. He did not respond. His body was very still, his eyes seemed to be looking far away to some very distant place. I began to wonder to myself, "Where is he now? His body appears to be here on this chair, but where is he? What space is he in? There, or here, or both places at once?"

In and out of time

Time is another important dimension in marriage. Sometimes partners are constantly out of synch with each other; they seldom share the same experience of time. In marriage, time measurement is often relative to the pleasure experienced or the sense of commitment to a task. The difference between a loving time and a boring time depends on the perceptions of the individuals involved. Time may seem to "fly" or "drag," depending on how partners experience it.

Time is usually thought of as chronological and linear, as that which can be measured by clock or calendar. "Be home on time," or, "Our anniversary is July 5," are common chronological reminders. Time has been measured in many ways—by the sun, moon, and stars, by sundials, by fire clocks, by mechanical clocks, and so forth. It has been standardized so that we can speak of Greenwich mean time or eastern standard time or daylight saving time.

Time is also measured in terms of movement in space: one day is the length of time it takes for the earth to make a complete rotation on its axis. Place is also often measured in terms of time, as when someone says, "It takes about six hours to drive from Los Angeles to San Francisco."

However, things are not always the way we experience them. For example, we see the star Sirius at a certain place in the sky, yet the light seen tonight from Sirius actually left there almost nine years ago. In the meantime, the star has moved, so it is not now where we see it.

Einstein discovered that time is relative. For example, if an astronaut in a spaceship increased his speed, his clock would run slower. He would not be aware of this until, returning to earth, he would discover that the length of his trip was not a few days, as he had thought, but a duration of some years.

In a marriage one partner may smile at the other, yet the smile may be the afterglow of a recent clandestine meeting with someone else rather than an expression of here-and-now affection. The person is really in a different time and space. An older couple might see each other through the rose-colored glasses of their courtship days rather than seeing each other in the present time.

The most essential and valuable kind of time is what I call *prime time.* During prime time, partners give their best to each other, focus on each other, speak the truth, and listen with love—in other words, they are truly present for each other. They are operating in the here and now, solving problems, sometimes developing intimacy, and responding to each other's needs and values. They don't have one eye on the TV or newspaper, or even one ear to the telephone or teapot. They are not off somewhere else in space.

In contrast to prime time, there is *leftover time,* often tainted with unsavory residues. Like polluted air or a body that needs bathing, leftover time is never fresh. It is what is left over at the end of a long day or after an arduous chore. In the kitchen, leftovers of well-kept foods are often tasty; leftovers of time seldom are. Their quality is never really sufficient to nourish a marriage. Many problems occur when partners continually give each other leftover time and save their prime time for others.

Another kind of time is what I call *challenging time.* A new problem arises or an old problem can no longer be ignored, and people are called on to respond. Some refuse to meet the challenge. Others do so because they recognize that the challenge has meaning and that finding a solution will give more vitality to life. This kind of time is often experienced during a crisis. But it can also involve a more extended period of life.

Upon retirement, for example, many older people settle into a rocking-chair routine. To them life has lost meaning; they ignore new challenges. Others, however, refuse to adopt a rocking-chair existence and instead continue hobbies or professions, or begin new careers or develop new interests. They meet the challenge of time and discover that life can be just as fulfilling in one's nineties as at earlier ages. By playing, loving, and working, they continue to find meaning for their lives. In a way, they are giving a new meaning to time. They have met the challenge of growing older.

In addition to these kinds of time, some people experience the sense of being "outside of time." The concept is not a new one, although different phrases have been used to describe the phenomenon. Being outside of time means transcending our customary experiencing of time. We are surprised, for example, to look at a clock and see that what seemed like seconds was really hours, or that what seemed like hours was really minutes.

An intense sexual experience often has an out-of-time dimension. This dimension may be different from prime time, which is focused, meaningful, and can be related to clock time. Often, a timeless experience is a taste of eternity, a spiritual experience of transcendent beauty. Like an out-of-body experience, it is difficult to describe.

When partners do not relate to time in the same way, or when they give different meanings to the time spent together, problems can occur. But partners can often help each other with time problems. A loving husband can move his wife out of the leftover time of a day's work to the prime time of a quiet dinner out. Sometimes one partner can help the other recognize that they are in a challenging time, that decisions must be made about placing an elderly parent in a nursing home or about changing role expectations or about planning how to live under new financial constraints. Understanding how your partner relates to time and what time zone he or she is in will help you support each other in an important dimension of your marriage.

Boredom

One of the least easily recognized, yet most frequent causes for marriage failure is the routine of everyday living. *Minor dissatisfactions continually occur.* Disagreements over money, recreation, friends, parents, in-laws, children, and stepchildren can wear couples out. Their dreams become tarnished, the romance disappears, the optimism and excitement of their early married years fades away.

One young husband complained, "I feel like I'm in a squirrel cage, going around and around, getting nowhere." His wife retorted, "You think you're bored, what about me? Dishes, diapers, dustpan. No fun. Never. If I'd known marriage was such a grind, I never would have gotten married."

Most people feel like prisoners, at one time or another, of the "daily grind." Grinding instruments can crush, shape, or sharpen. The slogan, "Keep your nose to the grindstone," means to keep working continuously, often at a routine task. Unlike a grinding wheel that sharpens a cutting edge, the daily grind often crushes the humanness of people, dulls the edges of their senses, dulls their dreams, and dulls their desire for romance and excitement. For most people, daily routines do not provide enough stimulation, freshness, or newness. When people are bored with each other they usually feel less involved; time drags when they are together and they often would rather be in another place. The boredom may be so pervasive that a person begins to cast about desperately for some excitement, perhaps an extramarital affair or a job outside the home.

Some people, however, actually prefer the predictability of one day being the same as the next. They feel safer or more comfortable when they can count on the many routines that give order to their existence. They still need excitement, but they find it in other ways: stimulation from a rich fantasy life, an intense intellectual life, or occasional vacations that enable them to "get away from it all" before resuming their routines.

When people with a high need for stimulation and change marry people who have a low need for these elements, conflict often erupts. Accusations fly: "You're always on the go. Don't you ever just want to relax?" "Sure I do, but not the same old tedious way, day after day." "Well, I like at least *some* consistency. You're never content." "And I thought you had a sense of adventure . . . what a mistake."

Minor unsolved problems are often spoken of as boring: "I'm so bored with that peeling wallpaper." "I'm so bored of never having enough money to *do* anything." "I'm so bored with every single article of clothing in my closet."

Many couples feel more bored "stuck" at home than when they go out, because they learned to feel this way when they were children. Children complain of boredom when kept inside the house with "nothing to do" and "no one to play with." And, if they don't find "something to do" inside that is interesting to them and acceptable to their parents, they may plead to "go outside and have some fun." If their parents exhibit indifference or seem preoccupied, the children may create some negative form of excitement simply to get any kind of attention, even if it takes the form of a scolding, for nothing is more painful to them than being totally ignored.

When such children grow up and get married, they may once again be bored at home. As a couple, they may know how to have fun in bed, but they may not know how to have any other kind of fun when inside the house. Their problems may seem so overwhelming that they have neither the time nor energy for laughter and joy. The old question of "what to do" may be answered with TV, a passive form of entertainment, or with more and more chores or hobbies or studies that keep them apart. Or, they may create a fight, so that once more they can get some attention. Finally, they may "go out to play" and get excitement and stimulation from someone else.

Boring jobs are often related to role expectancies. In many marriages the husband is expected to earn the money and the wife to keep the house. This is changing as more and more wives obtain jobs and more husbands are helping with household chores. Nevertheless, role expectancies remain constant, or at least linger to some extent, in the majority of marriages.

Commonly, people who work outside the home view those who work inside as having more freedom, more flexibility to structure their time as they please.

Resentment may build. Conversely, of course, the stay-at-home partner often feels bored and sees the spouse as "having all the excitement."

> *One woman complained, "He gets to travel all the time, entertains his customers at big lunches, has a sexy-looking secretary to fix his coffee. I'm just here in the same old grind." Her husband countered this with, "She has friends over every day and is always taking a new class in something. If she wants to just sit around and read a book she can. I have to be on the job, pushing myself and employees constantly. I wish I had it as good as she does."*

Comparisons and competitiveness on "my life is more boring than yours" do not reflect loving. "I'm so bored" often implies, "Tell me what to do for entertainment and excitement." "You're so boring" often implies, "You'd better be entertaining or else. . . ." Talking openly about one's feelings of boredom is a risk and thus takes courage, but it is certainly worth the struggle. Although seemingly a minor problem at first—perhaps just a small dissatisfaction reflected in sulking or angry behavior—boredom can escalate rapidly. It may lead to some kind of escape behavior or, if not confronted and solved, may result in separation or divorce.

Typical responses to problems

People commonly use one of five typical responses when faced with any kind of problem, be it a conflict of needs or values or a crisis.

One response to problems is *coping*. All people have some coping skills, the ability to remain stable while a problem runs its course. For example, persons may cope with illness while waiting for its symptoms to subside, or cope with grief while waiting for it to lessen, or cope with the boredom of the daily grind while waiting for a day off. They often are willing to do so because the activity has some meaning in itself or is a means to an end that has greater meaning. Coping with boredom often requires waiting for something to pass. It requires strength and determination to survive the wearing away of body, mind, or spirit.

Another response to problems is to *withdraw* physically or emotionally. Some people do this because they believe there's no solution. Others think, "It's not my problem." Others withdraw only temporarily by stepping back to gain a new perspective and a fresh point of view. Still others withdraw to collect more information before making a decision.

A third response is to *ignore* a crisis or to ignore the symptoms signalling an incipient crisis. A severe toothache may be a symptom that a dental crisis is about to occur. Sudden indifference of a spouse may be a symptom of an interpersonal crisis. Continuing criticism by one's partner may mean the same. People who think of themselves as patient, long-suffering, and able to endure a lot seldom act in response to the daily grind of small everyday irritations. They ignore the symptoms and may only recognize the problem when, for example, a spouse says, "I'm leaving."

The fourth response to crisis is to *attack* with words: "I'll tell him a thing or two. Nobody can do that to me," or, "I'll get even with you. Just wait and see." Approached in a more positive fashion, an attack tactic can often help solve a crisis. Many people, for example, have mobilized their will power, fought against serious illness, and won the fight. There are many couples who have experienced a crisis period in their marriage and have fought successfully to regain the love they believe in.

Becoming involved, out of the belief that people can and do change, is the fifth response. Becoming involved requires courage to face problems honestly and commit time and energy to solving them. It may mean giving up old ways of thinking; it may mean learning how to forgive.

Committing oneself to developing an intimate marriage means involving oneself in a full-time endeavor. An intimate, loving marriage is not the same as a friendly companionship of two people who, for the most part, go their separate ways. Being involved in a loving relationship motivates a couple to desire and strive for even more depth. They work toward that goal—together and individually. They are neither too hopeless nor too proud to seek outside help from marriage counselors or other professionals. They are aware and open about their sexual and emotional needs. They are not afraid to change, not afraid to confront their problems and attempt to solve them.

A six-step process for problem solving

A lot of people are skeptical of formulas and processes; they believe their situation too unique to be helped by a ready-made prescription. The following process, however, is general enough to be useful in most problem situations and flexible enough to meet differing needs. It has six steps: awareness of symptoms, defining the problem, exploring the options, making the decision, taking action, and evaluating the process and results.

Awareness of a problem usually starts with an awareness of the symptoms. Realization may come suddenly, as, for example, when one spouse packs up and moves out while the other is away on a business trip. Or, awareness may come gradually, as when one or both notice a growing disinterest in sexual expression or in being together in other ways. Both of these actions signal a desire to get away from or get rid of the other person.

Another kind of behavior that stimulates awareness is an escalation of conflict—more fights, more yelling or blaming, more defensiveness and more offensiveness. The problem is not the fighting or the withdrawal from each other. These are merely symptoms that something is wrong. The "something wrong" may be conflicting needs, views, or values.

The second step is *defining the problem.* This includes discovering how the problem began in the past and how it is evolving in the present. Whose needs are not being met? Whose views are being ignored? Which values are in collision?

In any marriage, the two people involved may be aware that something is wrong, but define the problem quite differently. One couple who came to me for counseling expressed great unhappiness. They were separated and considering divorce, yet many interests they had in common held them together. The major *symptom* was sexual problems; however, after talking awhile, they discovered that their real problem was one of conflicting needs.

John complained of being bored and unhappy. He wanted her to go to work, so that they could have more money and more material things. John traveled a lot as a business consultant and had a high need for stimulation and approval.

Jean, too, was unhappy, but not from being a housewife and mother. She enjoyed her role as homemaker, but was unhappy because she couldn't seem to please him. Continually criticized for not being lively, vivacious, and active in the business world, she had become more and more defensive, withdrawn, and scared.

It was partially their needs that were in conflict: he needed more excitement than she did; she enjoyed simplicity and quietness more than he. Originally this difference had actually attracted them to one another. Then, unconsciously, each tried to make the other conform to his or her own image.

Their views of marriage were also partially in conflict. To her, the primary importance was having a traditional home and family. To him, romance and excitement were primary.

Over the years, their arguments and actions were reinforced by repetition and became strongly held values. Ultimately, they were unable to perceive that their real problems were actually linked to the second step in the problem-solving process. They had not adequately defined their conflicting needs and views.

The third step in problem solving is *exploring the options.* "Brainstorming" is the best way to begin. When people brainstorm, they withhold judgment temporarily about what will and won't work and allow their imaginations and creativity free rein. It is a technique often used in company "think tanks" to find new solutions to old problems. All ideas are listed, regardless of how irrational or impractical the ideas may seem. It's fun, it's fast, it stimulates further creativity, and it often provides surprising solutions.

When brainstorming has run its course, it's time to become practical again and go back to reconsider the pros and cons of each option. Each option is weighed. If I move to a new job, what will it cost me in time, energy, money, and so on? What will it cost my family? If I don't move, what will not moving cost us both?

On the basis of this kind of evaluation, people take the fourth step, *making a decision on what to do.* Many individuals find this very difficult, especially if some kind of risk is involved and they fear not making the "right" choice. "I just *can't* decide" is a common lament. Or, if they do decide, they may complain, "I just don't feel *comfortable* with my decision."

Some people decide, then redecide time after time. Others procrastinate their decision making so long that their options disappear; the choice is made by another person or by a set of circumstances or simply by the passage of time.

Some kinds of decisions are much more stressful than others, for example, decisions that follow the death of a family member or decisions about divorce. Questions regarding the kind of funeral or the terms of a divorce settlement are usually tough ones, but so are the seemingly simpler decisions that follow, like what to do with the deceased's clothes or who gets the favorite rug. These are often more emotion-charged than the "business" arrangements of a crisis situation.

If people get over this hurdle of decision making and choose a plan to follow, it's time for the fifth step, *taking action.* Again, this is not a comfortable move, for it involves risk and possible rejection or failure. Taking action is so scary for some people that they become phobic and feel literally paralyzed. A phobia is an intense fear of some kind. Common phobias are the fear of meeting new people, fear of applying for a job, fear of speaking the truth, and fear of conflict.

A common cure for fear is desensitization, a specialized technique using imagination and visualization. If what is wanted is courage to leave the safety of a home and apply for a job, a person can sit down, relax, and visualize getting ready. If that feels comfortable, the person can visualize himself or herself going out the door. If that feels scary, the person returns to the earlier, safe fantasy. Gradually, through visualizing each new step before taking it, the phobia decreases. Action becomes possible.

Many actions that people take are possible steps to growth. Other actions may seem to be correct at the time, but later turn out wrong. When this happens, the actions or results can frequently be modified or reversed by other acts. A person may return to a former profession if a new career proves unsatisfactory. People may remarry when they discover their divorce was a mistake.

The sixth step is *evaluating the process and the results.* Each step in the process should be reviewed to determine whether something important was omitted and, if so, whether it now can be included. Evaluation involves measuring the joy and pain, the cost to self and the cost to others of the results achieved.

Sometimes the results of evaluation are positive and show love in action. Sometimes evaluation reveals that other problems remain, perhaps even more difficult ones, still needing to be solved. When problems escalate beyond a certain point, when they no longer seem "solvable," one or both partners may decide to fight it through or to let go. In a living marriage, it's just as important to know when to let go as when to hang on.

Fighting to hold on

At one time or another, almost every couple ends up fighting over their conflicting needs, views, or values. Most partners have "merry-go-round," repetitive fights or "gunnysack" resentments they have saved up for years. Most of these fights are not very constructive; they leave both partners feeling cheated and no problem solving is accomplished. Learning how to fight fairly is a skill that most people need to learn. With a fair fight, problems do get worked out and both partners can wind up the winners they were meant to be.

Yet many refuse to fight because they are afraid to speak up for themselves, or they're unwilling to speak the truth as they see it, or they back down from

their position prematurely. People who live by this pattern generally do so because they are afraid that, if they assert themselves, they might make a situation worse than it already is. In many cases, they are angry, although they may or may not be in touch with their anger. The anger and resentment they want to express outwardly may eventually be turned inward and show up in psychosomatic symptoms.

The opposite extreme is equally nonproductive. Some individuals approach conflict fully armed; they are out to win any battle, by fair means or foul. They are not assertive, they are aggressive. Like bulldozers, they run over other people's dreams, ridicule their values, and try to destroy their sense of worth.

Withdrawing from a fight is occasionally appropriate, as is fighting hard. However, to win by fighting "dirty," as sometimes happens in competitive sports, is really to lose. The words "fighting fair," on any playing field or in any other activity, imply sportsmanship, knowing the rules and observing them, not cheating, not playing out of turn, and so forth. A sporting conflict is not a gladiator battle, yet some couples act as if they'd like to kill each other, in one way or another.

When faced with conflict, partners need to ask themselves: What's at stake? What price will each of us have to pay? Is the issue important? Are the arguments realistic? Or is it all exaggerated because of our growing frustration? After these questions are answered, a couple needs to make an "appointment" to fight, specifying what the fight will be about. They *don't* select a time when one of them is sick, or on the way to work, or preoccupied with other pressing concerns. Although a fight can't be postponed indefinitely without becoming worse, the timing needs to be fair to both persons.

Elegance in fighting, according to George Bach, means never driving an opponent against the wall, and if a lightweight fighter is challenging a heavyweight, the lightweight should be allowed to choose the time when he or she feels strongest.[4] Recognizing this, each can fight for *understanding*—"I win, you win"—instead of engaging in a fight that results in the loss of esteem—"I win, you lose" or "I lose, you win." One wife complained that her husband yelled so much that she feared he would almost kill her. The husband retorted, "Oh, you and your soft voice—you say just what hurts the most."

Couples who truly want to solve their problems recognize that "hitting below the belt" is unfair. They are committed to the belief that honesty and candor are not the same as deliberate injury, that direct involvement is always a risk, and that marriage is for problem solving, which can be accomplished only in fair ways, not foul.

Grief and letting go

Much of life is filled with comings and goings, with loving and being loved, with leaving and being left. In the flow of life, partners need to learn how to let go. Yet many are haunted with the dilemma of when it's right to hang on and when it's time to let go. Hang on to those others, or let them go? Hang on to that dream, or let it go?

When partners refuse to fight *for* their marriage and fight primarily *against* each other, maybe that's the time to let go. How do you identify such people? George Bach characterizes them as those who will not "drop their masks and inhibitions and come out leveling," who cannot get their mates to enter into the process as a joint effort, who "take so many cocktails, sleeping pills, tranquilizers and wake-up pills that they never give their emotions a chance to unfold," and who are emotionally empty, yet think they have everything.

Sacrificing and sharing have little value to these people; their lives are lost in "chronic blandness, boredom, and economic 'success.' " They start to fight, then turn cold in "resignation or despair, instead of using the crisis as the starting point of an intensive and informed effort to help each other grow."[5]

The process of letting go requires that a person engage in what is called "grief work." This is a normal process of working through the grief, severing the past if it interferes unduly with the present, and experiencing new freedom to look toward the future with hope.

Grief work is needed whenever a person or a couple experiences some kind of loss. There are big griefs, as when a child is born retarded or a beloved person dies, and there are little griefs, as in giving up the dream of finding a perfect dress to wear to a party or of getting football tickets on the fifty-yard line. Small griefs are primarily disappointments. There are also medium-sized griefs, such as when a grownup son or daughter moves so far away that personal contact must be markedly reduced or when a job is lost or illness interferes with a lifestyle.

A large-sized grief to one person may represent only a small grief to another. A divorce case illustrates the difference.

> *Maureen was in love with her husband Peter and treasured their marriage; he believed himself to be in love with another woman. "I want out," he said, "I want another chance to be happy." Maureen had two basic kinds of grief work to do. She had to let go of her dream of a happy marriage and she had to let go of the man she loved. Peter had less grief work. He had let his dream die earlier. Now he was free of grief; he had done his work of letting go and was ready to move on to a new relationship.*

There are basic stages in grief work, according to Granger Westberg.[6] Not everyone goes through all of them or goes through them in this order. Yet each step is necessary.

Experiencing shock usually comes first. This acts much like a temporary anesthetic. The pain is numbed and the person often expresses something like, "I can't believe it." Shock may last a few minutes or many days. If it continues for months or years, professional help is needed.

Emotional release, the next step, is the most difficult for some people. Many in our culture, particularly men, have been taught to not show emotion. They may consciously hold back, or be unable to release, the tears of grief and/or the anger that usually accompanies them.

Feeling depressed and very lonely is another stage. Many people feel forsaken and unable to escape the black cloud of depression that surrounds them and obscures their vision. Loneliness may drive them into self-destructive behavior or into unhealthy new relationships.

Physical symptoms of distress (for example, headaches, insomnia, loss of appetite, stomach aches, and so forth) may come at this point or at any other time during the grief work. When people do not do their grief work, they may continue to suffer from psychosomatic symptoms for years because of some kind of loss.

Feelings of panic are also experienced, along with the inability to concentrate and the circular-type worrying that interferes with all effective functioning. At this stage, some people are distraught. They may even worry about going crazy.

Guilt is often common: guilt for what was done or not done, said or not said. Frequently the feelings of guilt are irrational and exaggerated, and may become neurotic.

Resentment and hostility often follow or accompany guilt. The individual blames others for the loss, finding fault with the doctor or the job or another person. Resentment may also take the form of tantrums, sulking, or trying to make others feel bad.

Feeling unable to get back to routine is one of the last stages, but one that may go on for years. If it does, it's unhealthy. Preoccupation with whatever or whomever has been lost often leads to physical feelings of weakness and vulnerability.

Emerging hope eventually begins to be felt. People at this stage look forward to the future—the next hour, day, or year. They see light at the end of the tunnel.

Adjustment to the loss is the final step. Persons who adjust do not stop caring, but they can and do start once more to love.

This Chinese love poem expresses the pain of lost love:

> *Over and over you told me, "We shall grow old together. Together at the same time, your hair and mine will turn white as the snow on the mountains, white as a summer moon." Today, Seignior, I have learned that you love another, and with broken heart I come to say adieu.*

> *One last time let us pour the same wine into our two cups. One last time sing to me the song which tells of the dead bird under the snow; then I will set sail on the river Yu Cheu, whose waters divide and flow to the east and to the west.*
>
> *Why are you weeping, young girls about to marry? Perhaps you will marry a man with a faithful heart, a man who will tell you sincerely over and over, "We shall grow old together."*[7]

Everyone has grief work to do, whether it's letting go of a dream, an expectation, a treasured possession, or an important relationship. Letting go is necessary, so that new ties of intimacy can develop—new dreams, new possessions, new expectations, new relationships. Letting go is a major step in achieving freedom, and it always requires courage. In a loving marriage, the step toward freedom and intimacy is worth the risk.

Chapter 7

"Why does the phone have to ring just at this moment?"

"Don't answer it."

"But it might be the girls, wanting to come home early."

"They're ten and twelve years old. I think they could wait ten minutes."

"Now the phone has stopped ringing."

"Will you stop worrying? We sent them to the movies just so we could have time alone."

"I know. Actually, I forget about time when your arms are around me like this."

"Me too."

Intimacy in Marriage

Some couples talk of intimacy as if it related exclusively to sex. Others talk about feeling intimate when they work together or solve problems together. Still others don't talk about intimacy at all. They may not know it exists or may not want it. As one corporation executive expressed it, "Intimacy—who wants it! It's too demanding, takes too much time."

Some people avoid all forms of intimacy. In a sacramental marriage intimacy may be avoided because one or both partners are afraid it would interfere with dedication to God. In a marriage for convenience a couple may avoid sexual intimacy because it takes time and energy away from the children or the job or because they fear an unwanted pregnancy. In a romanticized marriage intimacy is often a euphoric facade to disguise an overdependent relationship.

It takes courage to risk intimacy, as well as time and effort. But intimate relationships are what marriage is all about.

Four kinds of intimacy

In a course for married couples, the participants were asked what was most important to them, what they thought the positive "glue" was that held them together. Their responses fell into four categories of intimacy: values held in common, intellectual sharing and excitement, emotional support, and sexual closeness.

Intimacy in marriage is experienced as closeness, warmth, openness, and trust. When intimacy lacks these elements, so-called sexual intimacy may be merely intercourse—the adroit use of mechanics and techniques. Emotional intimacy may be merely overdependence—using the other person to escape a basic sense of insecurity. Intellectual intimacy may become a form of mind rape. The intimacy of shared values may only mask a self-righteous "we" feeling.

The values people hold in common pull them together. This is the reverse of having values that conflict. Common values lead to positive rather than negative feelings and create a warm, growing climate of intimacy.

One couple said it was religious values that were most important and kept them together. "That is part of what our church teaches," they said, "to be married, have a family, and to serve God as a family."

Another couple reported, "The most important thing in our marriage is that we *value* so many of the same things. For example, our children are top priority with both of us. We both like music, too. In fact, we made a lot of sacrifices to get a good stereo system. We went without movies, new clothes, and going out to dinner for a whole year to save the money. Some of our friends just go out and buy things and charge them. We don't. We don't want to be bogged down with all those payments. If we pay as we go, we have more financial freedom, and we certainly value that!"

These two couples had values that they agreed they shared. They were committed to their values. When other things occasionally went wrong in their marriage, the values they held in common pulled them back to each other.

Intellectual intimacy is closeness at the thinking level with an open sharing of ideas. It thrives in an atmosphere of freedom—freedom to express differences of opinion without being put down or ridiculed. Intellectual intimacy may also develop when partners work their way through a conflict of ideas or values to a new agreement or commitment.

It is not unusual for people to be attracted to other people "for the way they think." Frequently in college classes or in stimulating, creative jobs, one thinker is attracted to another. This intellectual attraction may even be stronger than emotional or sexual attractions. Often it leads to marriage. Sometimes it continues to be a major force in the marriage, sometimes not.

One young couple, excited over physics in graduate school, spent most of their free time talking about the theories and applications of physics. After they got married they continued to discuss their scientific interests. Their marriage was one of companionship, and they enjoyed their intellectual life together more than their sexual life.

When partners do not grow intellectually, when they refuse to rethink their beliefs, their intellectual intimacy may disappear. It is not uncommon for one partner in a marriage to grow intellectually while the other person remains "as is." In this kind of marriage, when important social, economic, and political issues come up on TV or in a social group, the growing partner is likely to be interested and involved. The other may be indifferent, bored, and tempted to retreat into fantasy or some other isolated activity.[1]

Intellectual intimacy is fostered when both partners are alert and interested in the world around them. They need not explore the same areas. Don is involved in local politics, while Gretchen is turned on by marine biology. But both have alert, inquiring minds and each enjoys the other's intellectual enthusiasm. They share their interests with each other, and each can depend on the other to be receptive to new ideas. Their intellectual companionship flourishes as each encourages the other with respect and honesty.

Emotional intimacy is openness and closeness at the feeling level rather than the thinking level. Couples who have developed emotional intimacy can transact in many ways—they laugh together, take care of each other, feel safe to say what they want to say.

One of the best ways to expand emotional intimacy is to improve communication between partners. If both think more about *listening to* than *being listened to,* their communication improves dramatically. Emotional intimacy grows when two people take time to listen to each other, to care about the other's feelings, and to guard their relationship. Sometimes this means setting aside time to discuss problems at work or at home, to discover how a partner is coping on a day-to-day basis. More often it is just remembering to say, "I hear you."

"Please take time to listen to me," is the plaintive plea in many marriages. But learning to listen to others is often difficult. It is a skill that is not taught in schools, as speech making often is.

The roots of poor listening often go back to childhood. For example, many homes teach negative listening. An admonition such as "I told you to listen to me, and you'd better do it" actually teaches the child to turn off and tune out, or to give the parent less than complete attention. Negative listening is also taught by parents who do not listen when their children try to tell them things.

Some children treated this way may decide to become silent and secretive, withholding their thoughts and feelings from others (after all, "No one will listen"). Others may decide to keep on talking, trying to be heard ("If I talk more, maybe someone might listen").

Overly verbal people are often poor listeners themselves. As grown-ups they may ramble on and on, so busy talking that they are unaware of their listener's responses. Other people may talk too much for a different reason: they were trained in childhood to report everything. Their parents frequently demanded, "Tell me everything that happened today." When grown up, these people may be so preoccupied with marshalling all the details of what happened that they, too, may not listen well to others.

When people are listened to, they feel accepted. Because they feel accepted, they feel freer to be their true selves and are less rejecting of others. Because they are less rejecting and see "the best" in others, they help partners become liberated and enjoy doing it. As Dag Hammarskjold wrote: "The Lover desires the perfection of the Beloved—which requires, among other things, the liberation of the Beloved from the Lover."[2]

To affirm other persons' individuality is generally to accept people as they are and to know that they are always in the process of becoming more of what they can be. True emotional intimacy involves an eagerness for the growth of the other person—not continually offering solutions, or advice, or information. It is to encourage the other person to think and do.

This kind of encouragement frequently happens when one person listens with respect to the other—listens to their feelings as well as their words—and does not respond with many words unless asked. It often means setting aside one's own thoughts and feelings to concentrate on the other. It means giving up a correcting stance of, "I'm right and you're wrong." Trying to set the other person straight is not a loving act of listening. Emotional intimacy grows with creative, sensitive listening.

Sexual intimacy is oneness at the physical level, a sharing of joy in each other's bodies and their union. But it is not easy to achieve. Four out of five couples who seek marriage counseling, it has been estimated, complain of sexual problems. "All he wants is to get it over with." "She takes too long." "It's boring." These kinds of comments point to a lack of true intimacy, in which there is a sense of freedom, a willingness to get involved and risk intensity. People who enjoy sexual intimacy honor each other and risk speaking the truth in love.

Sexual intimacy is not the same as sexual fidelity. Many couples claim they are committed to sexual fidelity, yet there may be little or no sexual intimacy in their relationship. They may act proud of their fidelity but have little love for each other. They may remain "true to each other" out of a sense of duty or fear rather than choice.

People like this may tease and entice others they are not married to. If another responds sexually, the teaser may retreat with: "Oh, I didn't mean *that*! I just wanted to flirt and have a little fun. Actually, I'm always true to the person I married."

Other couples are not committed to sexual fidelity. They may speak of their partner as being the "primary relationship," and although those words sometimes imply a sexual intimacy, usually they don't. Evaluating basic needs in relation to sex is one way to increase sexual intimacy.

Many marriages are high in one kind of intimacy and lower in another kind. In sacramental unions, for example, sexual intimacy may or may not be part of the marriage. In romantic unions, sex is often rated high, while intellectual intimacy with an exchange of ideas may be low. Day-to-day companionship may be lacking in a romantic union. Sexual intimacy may not be part of a marriage that is based on the convenience of family life and children. Emotional intimacy can be very satisfying, however, if both partners love their children and share similar values for them. In companionship marriages, sexual intimacy is often low, but emotional and intellectual intimacy may be very high. In marriages for loving, the partners experience all four kinds of intimacy.

By far the most thought-about kind of intimacy in a marriage is sexual intimacy. It is what sets marriage apart from other kinds of intimate relationships based on the sharing of values, emotions, or intellectual interests. For that reason, after we look at barriers to intimacy, we shall devote the rest of our discussion on intimacy to sexual intimacy and how to use it to make your marriage more loving.

Barriers to intimacy

People are frustrated by many barriers to intimacy—yet most are self-imposed to avoid closeness. Martha, a young woman who had been married twice, explained the paradox this way:

> *Ever since my father died suddenly when I was four years old, I've been afraid to get close to men. It's as though some part of me almost expects them to go away. Besides my two marriages, I have had several important affairs, and my lovers always leave when I don't expect it. Maybe I pick out those kinds of men—men who will leave me. Maybe I do something to kind of push them out. I wish I knew. I want to be close, and also I don't want to be close.*

The loss of a parent by death, desertion, or divorce is frequently a traumatic experience to children. When grown up, such people may avoid loving and getting close *because they fear that they will be left alone once more.* The fear of being physically hurt, as well as emotionally hurt, is a similar barrier to any kind of closeness and intimacy. This fear may also start in childhood.

Many people feel anxious *because they lack a firm sense of personal or sexual identity.* This confusion usually begins at an early age. It is in comments such as, "I just don't know who I really am" or "All my life I've wondered what it would be like to be the opposite sex."

Other people avoid closeness in marriage *because they are afraid their faults will be discovered* and their partner will find out how "bad" they are. This "badness" is often a fantasy, an exaggeration of their own imperfections and mistakes.

Other common feelings that marriage partners may be afraid to reveal are *anger, hostility, and resentment.* Some people are so full of anger that they are afraid of exploding if they begin to release it. So they "keep their distance." Keeping one's distance is easy to do in this kind of world. Getting sick provides one way. Being sad or preoccupied is another. Overworking and getting tired are sure barriers to intimacy.

One of the strongest blocks to intimacy is *bringing past resentments and past expectations into the present.* The past may be an earlier event in the marriage: "On our honeymoon you just went to sleep." It may be contact with a previous mate or lover that keeps resentment high: "You promised you'd never see her again." The most frequent block to intimacy is projecting an image of a parent onto the marriage partner. The projection may be some of the good parenting received in childhood, or some of the bad. Carl Jung claimed that people project both good and bad parenting onto their partner.

Richard's father maintained emotional distance by continually withdrawing behind the newspaper or bottle or into the garage to fuss with his tools. He was insecure himself and did not know how to get close to others. Richard's mother was more outgoing and nurturing. When Richard married Claire he wasn't aware he was choosing a partner who combined qualities of both his parents—often she withdrew; often she was nurturing. Richard liked the nurturing but became so angry when she withdrew or withheld herself from him that he got a divorce. Unfortunately, he married someone else who did just the same. It took years before he could "own" his part of the problem and see how his projections and expectations encouraged this behavior in others.

Unresolved conflicts with childhood friends and brothers and sisters can be another major block to intimacy. Feelings of competitiveness, rivalry, jealousy, may pervade the marriage. One or both partners want to prove superiority and often will go to great lengths to do so. When one feels no longer superior, he/she tends to sulk like the six-year-old child who says, "I won't play with you anymore," or gets angry and throws the checkers in frustration.

My husband comes from a large family. He and his five brothers and sisters were all involved in competitive sports. I did not have this experience, so, like a spectator on the bleachers, I tend to sit and observe people who enjoy organized sports. "Come on," he would say encouragingly, "learn how to play golf." "Learn how to play chess."

I worked on learning chess. Even bought books to study. I didn't enjoy it. It was so intense, this almost-silent competition, that it was no fun. Then I learned golf. That was better. Not that I became a great golfer. No way! It was just that I like being outside walking, talking, exercising, and listening to the meadowlarks. At last I am a medium-to-fair golfer. My husband, however, is almost a "pro." I'm no competition for him, so he plays with his men friends weekly when he wants to express the competitive part of his personality and with me when he wants to express his nurturing side. "Great shot, Muriel!" he'll yell, even when it may not be. Competitiveness as a block to intimacy does not seem to be part of our marriage. Perhaps that is why we are freer than some couples to grow individually in our own ways and to grow closer in our loving.

Another block to intimacy that may come from the past and interfere with the present is the role expectancies of what a husband and wife "should" be and do. Often a couple has role expectancies that are strongly held values—and conflicting. When they are, emotional intimacy, as well as the intimacy that comes with shared values, is blocked.

Pauline's father died when she was young, so her mother learned how to make household repairs and taught her the basic skills as well. Pauline married Ted, a man who was competent with tools and expected repairs to be part of his role as husband. When she sometimes repaired things without waiting for him or consulting him, he felt angry and would shout, "Why couldn't you wait until I got home?" She would feel confused, "I don't understand you. Why should I wait when I had time to do it?"

Part of Ted's unspoken value system was that he would do repairs and, in doing so, feel important. He accused Pauline of competing for "the male role." Not until he became aware of her childhood experiences with repairing was he freer to evaluate role values and not be threatened by her competence.

In a less healthy marriage, couples like Pauline and Ted might (1) become rigid, insisting that the other person change attitudes, (2) refuse to discuss the matter and continue as before, or (3) withdraw with, "I'll never try to help you again." To confront and sometimes change role expectancies is a risk that requires courage and hope. But it's worth the risk, because it can lead to new freedom, add new excitement, and release more energy that can lead to further intimacy.

A major block to sexual intimacy is the negative training that many people experience in childhood. Since the beginning of time, many parents have believed and have taught their children that sexuality is animalistic, indecent, or only for procreation. Consequently, children have grown up confused by inaccurate information, or brainwashed into thinking sex is distasteful, something to be avoided, a necessary evil. They have learned not to feel sexy, talk sexy, or even think sexy.

Some people, when they think sexy, fantasize being with someone else. Doing this seems to release their potency and inhibitions. But fantasizing someone else when having intercourse with a marriage partner is a sure way to destroy emotional intimacy. Sex then becomes a convenient way to reduce tension or build up a lonely fantasy life, instead of a loving way to increase intimacy.

Sexy thinking, talking, and feeling can enhance most marriages. If you are not comfortable with this idea, you can take steps to change your attitude. With your partner, you can decide to do it and learn to enjoy it. Understanding sensuality, sexuality, and eroticism could be your first step in a sexual affirmation plan.

Sensuality and eroticism

People are born sensory creatures—hearing, seeing, tasting, touching, smelling, and intuiting. It is part of being human. To be sensuous is to be susceptible to the senses and to feel pleasure through them.

Some people try to avoid sensuousness. They deny themselves the pleasures that come from eating a delightful meal, listening to good music, touching soft skin, looking at an expressive face, or enjoying the scent of perfume.

They don't enjoy their bodies. In fact, they seem embarrassed even to have them. If they don't like the way they look, they may dress and undress in the dark. If they don't like the way their bodies feel, they try to ignore messages from their bodies. Some people even try to "hold back" the need to urinate. They feel embarrassed to leave a social or business situation to go to the bathroom.

People who deny their bodies to this degree may not eat, drink, or exercise properly to maintain good health. They may expect their bodies to function like machines that don't need attention. They may allow situational anxiety, or overwork, to interfere with their dreaming and sleeping patterns; they may be tired and frustrated and do nothing about it. A distaste for the body and a denial of its human needs blocks sensual enjoyment and frequently leads to a denial of sexuality.

Touching and being touched can be a most effective sensuous, sexual "turn on"—or a most effective sexual "turn off." Many people have their own desires for specific kinds of touching. Some like to be fondled, some don't. Some like gentleness; some like roughness. Some prefer certain parts of their bodies to be touched and not other parts; some enjoy touch on their entire body. The relatively new and widespread use of massage has helped many couples get in touch with a desire for sensuality they didn't know they had.

It's important to discover or rediscover sensuality in your marriage—both yours *and* your partner's. Enjoying your mutual sensuality can foster new sexual intimacy. Later in this chapter are some ideas that will help lead you in that direction.

When related to sexuality, sensuousness is called eroticism. The word *erotic* comes from the Greek word *eros.* If something is erotic it is intended to arouse sexual desire; people, literature, and other forms of art can all be erotic.

In affluent cultures eroticism is often encouraged in many forms. In cultures where existence is marginal because of poverty, eroticism may be frowned upon. In repressive cultures, such as ancient Rome, eroticism may be illegal. When this is the case, it often becomes more attractive.

Clothes, perfumes, lotions, and other externals are often used for erotic purposes. The popular purchase of black lacy lingerie at Christmas, often by husbands for their wives, indicates the desire to be stimulated afresh. Men also have their own vanities to stimulate women. After-shave lotions are appealing. Jackets with padded shoulders make men look bigger, seemingly more virile. From about 1400 to 1600, it was the fashion in some parts of Europe for men to wear tight breeches with a bag in front inside the pants. It was not uncommon for the bag to be stuffed with something extra to indicate large sexual organs. The purpose was to excite the observers' fantasies, much as padded bras are used by some women today.

A certain way of walking or sitting can also be erotic. Some people flirt with their eyes to stimulate sexual desire in the other person. Others pinch or bite for the same purpose.

A way of speaking may also be sexually stimulating, therefore erotic. Some people are aroused by the use of slang words that refer to intercourse. Others "turn on" with dirty jokes or other forms of verbal stimulation.

Most newstands carry a large supply of erotic "pin-up girl" magazines. The photographs are to stimulate the male reader, if only into sexual fantasies. A similar type of magazine designed for women has not proven successful. Women tend to want romance.

Eroticism is often an important element in those marriages that are for sexual convenience or for romance. Eroticism increases desire for the people involved. Couples feel warmer and sexier, the men more potent, the women more passionate.

Currently, a number of popular books are designed to teach people how to be sexier and more erotic so they can stimulate themselves and their partners more effectively. Salvation through sex is preached in every form of advertising by the new evangelists who, in their efforts to sell everything from mouthwash to pantyhose, promise sexual paradise if you use their products.

Pornography is a step beyond eroticism. Usually, it is writings, cartoons, or pictures designed to excite lascivious feelings. Some people are excited by pornography; others are repulsed by it. Instead of turning on, they turn off. An attractive wife explained it this way:

> *Sam likes those dirty movies and insists that I go with him to see them. Afterward he wants sex in weird ways. I feel as if he wants me to be a prostitute to give him a bunch of jollies. But I'm not one. I used to feel loving and very sexy, but now I'm feeling like a sex machine.*

It is a short step from pornography to sadomasochism. The use of children for sex and the physical brutalizing of adults before or during intercourse are the two most common forms of sadomasochism. Sadomasochism expresses both self-hatred and hatred of the partner. Anyone who gets his or her "kicks" from inflicting or receiving pain can probably benefit from exploring the underlying reasons for it. Yet people like this often feel so guilty or embarrassed that they do not seek help until a crisis occurs. It does not have to be that way. The intensity *can* be redirected toward loving.

Plutarch, at the beginning of the Christian era, pleaded for love to accompany sex. He wrote:

> *It is true that sex without love is like hunger or thirst; it is mere satisfaction of a need and leads nowhere. . . .*
>
> *On the contrary, physical union with a wife is a source of friendship, a sharing together in a great mystery. Sensual delight is brief, but it is like a seed from which day by day there grow between husband and wife consideration for each other, kindness, tenderness, and confidence.*[3]

Plutarch's idea was new and strange in that period of history. The same idea would still feel new and strange for some couples today.

Sexual tension and the five views of marriage

Tension and contraction, satisfaction and relaxation are part of most marriages. Without tension a marriage may be boring. Without some kind of satisfaction, the marriage may collapse.

Tension is felt in many ways—intellectually, emotionally, physically. For example, intellectual tension may occur between two people who differ on politics, on how to rear children, or on how to spend money. If considerable energy is used from an "I'm right, you're wrong" position, emotional tension usually emerges. At the same time bodies may keep score of the tension and stress and respond by changed breathing patterns or pulse rate.

Sexual desire is a biological instinct that often creates considerable tension. How people deal with this tension depends on their view of marriage. In a sexually convenient marriage, the partners may experience tension primarily in the genitals; often this can be satisfied with orgasm and ejaculations. Such people do not believe that the afterglow and "pillow talk" are especially important.

Tension often develops between people who have a spiritual view of marriage. They may try to ignore and transcend their physical desires. They may speak of themselves as "above that kind of thing," as being interested only in the religious aspects of life. It is not uncommon for such people to experience tension headaches and the reduction of tension may occur only with drugs.

Romantic partners, when sexually frustrated, often experience stomach discomfort. They may say they "have trouble eating," and may not be able to digest what they do eat. But all tension seems to fall away when the idealized other person becomes emotionally or sexually available and the longing and stress are reduced.

Companionship is frequently thought of as a connection of one mind to another. Sexual tension in this kind of marriage may be so low that the partners feel satisfied after a long, intense conversation or a walk in the rain or some other shared interest.

In a loving, holistic marriage, partners relieve tension by the intimate sharing of sexual wants and needs, by touching, by caring, by commitment to the other person. Love, strangely enough, is often said to be an affair of the heart. In a marriage of many years, one partner may die shortly after the other. Friends interpret this as "dying of a broken heart."

The need for a sexual affirmation plan

The happiest lovers are those who use their sexual tension and power to help create sexual and emotional contentment in their partners and who, at the same time, feel contented themselves.

During the climax of the sexual act, the boundaries of the personality may seem to dissolve, and one may have a sense of merging with the other person or with the infinite. Ecstasy seems to transcend humanness. For many, it is a spiritual experience. Learning how to enjoy and heighten sexual intimacy is what a sexual affirmation plan is all about.

Each couple needs to develop their own plan based on their likes and dislikes. Any plan needs to include (1) a heightening of sensory awareness, (2) an updating of information with increased thinking and planning, (3) an evaluation of traditions, past experiences, and prejudices that aid or hinder sexual enjoyment, and (4) a decision or redecision that sexual intimacy is important and is definitely related to intercourse.

Without these aspects, intercourse may be seen as a duty or may become casual and without love or passion. Charlene, who came for counseling, described how duty and casualness fit together for her.

> *Well, it's Saturday night again and he'll expect me to act like a firecracker popping off. I don't feel I have much choice. It's my duty so I put on a big act for him. I'll wear a shorty nightgown, high heels, and wiggle my hips a lot. At a deeper level I don't care. We're just doing what books say to do, acting like we're in some dumb whorehouse porno movie. He may* act *like the big, tough stud when really it's such a* casual *way to pass time. The whole thing is a "put on" because we really don't care.*

Casual sex—either in or outside marriage—is a denial that intercourse is an important way to express love. Casual sex is sought by people who believe orgasm is only for the convenience of reducing tension. Casual sex inevitably becomes boring. Those involved get less and less pleasure and less and less excitement from it. It is a way to pass time, but they often conclude they "can take it or leave it." Couples frequently become disinterested in each other. The thrill is gone. The process is routine. A cough in the groin doesn't make up for the overwhelming delight of sex in a loving marriage.

The current increase of casual sex and "open" marriage has greatly reduced the number of people who believe in romance and love. No longer is one person "special," to be adored, to be courted and cared for. True, physical tension may be released sexually, yet emotional involvement with the partner is lacking.

When sexual intensity is lost and emotional involvement drops, some people withdraw from other forms of intimacy, others redirect their energy toward jobs, social life, children, hobbies and so forth. Still others begin a frantic chase for new stimulation that they may have once known and lost.

I believe that sexual intercourse is meant to be fun, exciting, creative and intense. If not disrupted by illness or prejudice, sexual energy continues into old age and may be just as fulfilling at age sixty as in the days of youth.

When people recognize that their sexual life is inadequate, and when they want to develop a sexual affirmation plan, courage is needed. It is a courageous act to admit to oneself and one's partner, "My body gets cold when you touch me because I'm afraid I'll be left high and dry," or, "I turn off when you smell all sweaty and need a shower," or, "For me, your perfume is revolting," or, "Touch me gentle, not like a batch of bread dough," or, "I don't know much about your body. I never see it," or, "I'm ashamed to tell you what I like," or, "Things my mother said about sex still seem to interfere with my letting go," or, "Can we try something new just to see what it's like?," or, "Maybe we should take a course in anatomy."

A knowledge of anatomy and how sexuality is affected by the six senses is necessary information for couples who want to improve and affirm their sexual intimacy.[4] Currently scores of books and sex manuals are available that discuss sexual anatomy. I suggest that everyone read a number of these books, more than just one or two. Becoming aware of different information and different points of view increases understanding and helps free partners from outmoded parental prejudices and archaic childhood training. The anatomy for loving is a marvelously complicated arrangement and knowing about it is vital to enhancing sexual intimacy.

Greater sensory awareness

Sexuality begins with an awareness of the senses and how partners can use them in a sexual affirmation plan. *Touch* is the primary sense; it is also an end in itself. Ashley Montague commented, "Babies, as well as adults, know the difference between being stroked the right way and being rubbed the wrong way."[5] When touch is loving, there is no rubbing the wrong way—out of indifference, ignorance, or lust. Each partner touches to please—sometimes gently, sometimes firmly. Never to hurt, only to add to pleasure.

Pleasure from touch is not limited to the genital area. Sexuality is diffused throughout the body. Although some zones are more sensitive than others, skin touch of nongenital areas increases intimacy. Studies by H. Harlow with monkeys showed that the pleasure of bodily contact with a soft, warm, cloth figure was even more important to them than feeding.[6] Other studies show that, for humans, skin touch may be even more important because of a special warmth. The skin absorbs and emits infrared rays at just the right wave-length to best affect another person's skin.[7]

Many couples do not have enough waking time to make up for the years of not having enough gentle skin touch. The problem is clear, the solution simple. They need a plan to make up for the deficit. The easiest one is to sleep nude. This will give six to eight hours, out of every twenty-four, for the comforting reassurances of bodily contact. It seems to heal people at deep levels of their psyche.

After touch, the next sense to bring into fuller awareness is *hearing*—of all kinds of sounds. The meadowlark outside, the rain on the roof, the soft stereo in the background, the creak of the floorboards (or the bedsprings), the words, the gasping, the moans—all can be affirmed as sensory background to sexuality.

Some couples with children limit the intensity of their intercourse because they are afraid of being overheard. Sex is normal and sometimes noisy. Therefore, any plan a couple develops needs to take into consideration the value they place on privacy. Waiting until the children or other relatives are asleep is seldom the best way to solve the problem, since fatigue from a long day's work often interferes with sexual excitement. When this is a pattern, some couples use the simple technique of going to bed early, then waking up early so they can meet sexually with new high energy from a deep night's sleep. Other couples sacrifice financially, so that they can have "a night on the town" and the freedom of a motel room.

The sense of *smell* is also important. The smell of massage oil or perfume, flowers, bath oil, scented candles, even the pungent pines close outside the window, all can add to the pleasure of sex. So can fresh body odors and a minty toothpaste mouth.

Body odors that are not pleasing can interfere with any sexual affirmation plan. As some people are more sensitive to odors than others, this is a subject that the partners may need to talk about. One of the functions of the skin is to act as an excretory organ. Therefore, the total body skin, as well as the genital area, needs to be kept clean.

In my work as a marriage counselor, it is not uncommon to hear one partner complain about the skin or mouth odor of the other. Emotional illnesses, as well as physical illnesses, sometimes increase this problem. Deodorant and similar products may help, but the illness itself needs to be healed before the person can smell healthy.

Bad breath and stale perspiration may not be sufficient reason for divorce, yet such things can interfere with loving sexuality. If a person has these hygiene problems and does not change them, one partner may decide the other partner "only wants sex" and is not interested in emotional intimacy. A sexual affirmation plan needs to consider the sensitivity of each partner's nose.

The sense of *taste*—a juicy orange, a well-prepared dinner, a picnic of wine, cheese, and bread—is often associated with eating. Taste can also be part of the total sex act. In a sexual affirmation plan, the taste of a mouth when kissing, or of skin or genitals, adds an erotic element to the total sexual experience for many couples. "I love nibbling on her ear," claimed one husband, "it tastes so good." His wife responded, "Of course, I can't taste my ear, but I know for sure how sexy you get when you do it."

As with smelling, a clean skin and mouth are more likely to have an appealing taste than when they are covered with daily grime or stale cigarette smoke.

Seeing the human body is one of the most beautiful experiences on earth. Each body is unique. One may look more like a Greek god or goddess than another. One may look like a "twig" and another like a plump succulent. One may be short and another tall. Yet each is beautiful, or potentially so.

Standards of beauty change, of course. The perception and definition of a beautiful body differs according to culture, subculture, historical era, and so forth.

What excites people sexually is sometimes related to what they saw in their childhood. Dangling gypsy earrings may act as a sexual stimulant to one person, tight pants to another. These objects may be imprinted on the mind and become fetishes, which are so interesting that the fetish is the attraction instead of the person wearing the fetish. Imprinting from childhood affects automatic visual responses later in life. Eric Berne writes:

> *In imprinting, the young bird will get turned on to a visual image of a certain form and color and respond to the object, which may be merely a piece of cardboard, as though it were its mother. It has no decision or free choice in the matter; it is torqued in by a certain stimulus and responds automatically. The stimulus may be only a silhouette, but the effect is full-bodied. In the same way, confronted with a turn-on, many people must give up the illusion that their feelings make sense and are proper to their being, because this is an automatic response.*[8]

Any sexual affirmation plan needs to use visual stimuli from time to time to enhance sexuality. Many men speak of themselves as "breast men" or "leg men" and may be more attracted by these parts of anatomy than other parts. In a loving marriage, wearing a low-cut blouse or a partially split skirt may be an erotic gesure that indulges these preferences without demeaning the person.

Many women comment on a man's height, shoulders, or hair. Perhaps their glances toward men drop lower on the body only when they think no one is watching. Or perhaps the cut of men's clothing is not quite as revealing as women's, so women focus their sight higher. A beard excites some women. Careful hair styling or a smooth shaven face interests others.

The shape of the partner's body or the way clothes, hair, or make-up is worn are not the only visual stimuli that add pleasure or displeasure to sex. Facial expression, movement, including how the partner walks, sits, crosses the legs, and so forth, are all part of the total picture. So, too, is the room where the couple makes love. The colors, the furniture, the pictures, the total decor may turn the couple on or turn them off. In any marriage, designing the background to enhance sensory pleasure can be an important part of the overall plan.

Intuition is the sixth sense. Many couples use theirs without awareness. For example, the selection of a partner is often an intuitive choice. A person may also intuit what to say and do to turn someone on sexually, or to turn them off.

Some couples block the use of their intuition and, by doing so, make many errors of judgment. Yet the use of intuition, along with creative thinking, is a personal resource all people have and often need to develop.

Being intuitive is popularly called having "hunches." Berne believes a hunch is knowledge based on experience and acquired through sensory contact with the subject, without the "intuiters" being able to explain to themselves or others exactly how they arrived at their conclusions.[9]

The hunches people have are not always trustworthy. They can be inaccurate because of what is called projection, a defense mechanism against unpleasant feelings. Projection includes attributing unacceptable urges and emotions to other persons. In marriage, one partner may "read into" the other partner his or her own feelings and interpretations. Shirley may accuse Ned with, "You don't want to be close to me and have sex tonight," when actually she might want some distance and not know it. Projection constantly operates in daily life—either normally or abnormally. If abnormal, it tends to be expressed as paranoid delusions.

In a sexual affirmation plan, distinguishing between intuition and projection is not always easy. However, it is often necessary. One way to do this is to ask yourself, before making an accusation, "I wonder if I am fantasizing about the other person what I really am or feel myself?"[10] Another way to sort out projection from intuition is: first to be quiet for a minute or two and relax, then to consciously stop thinking and let your internal antennae scan the situation without making any judgments. The next step is picking up, ideally by intuition, the "vibes" your partner is sending out. Then comes the feedback: "My hunch is you'd like me to take more initiative with you sexually. Is that right?" If your partner responds, "Yes, that's right," then intuition has probably been active.

Thinking and planning

A sexual affirmation plan requires more than the awareness and use of senses. It also requires a couple to use their minds to think, and on the basis of thinking, to plan.

Many couples, when confronted with sexual problems such as impotence, frigidity, disinterest, fear, and so forth try to solve them by logical thinking. They may set goals, process information, make plans. Sometimes, this way of thinking works. The following series of logical questions can be part of any sexual affirmation plan:

> *What about this woman (this man) turns you on?*
>
> *What about this woman (this man) turns you off?*
>
> *What do you want more of?*
>
> *What do you want less of?*
>
> *Are there external problems that worry you and interfere with your masculine (feminine) feelings of sensuousness?*
>
> *Can they be solved, or can they be temporarily set aside?*
>
> *Is there a physical problem that needs consideration?*
>
> *Do you need to be better informed?*
>
> *Are you playing some old negative memory tapes that interfere with a good sex life?*
>
> *What is your pay-off in replaying them?*
>
> *Are there words, gestures, actions that you could use to turn on your spouse?*
>
> *Would this behavior hurt or discount either of you?*[11]

Sometimes logical thinking alone does not work. Then creative thinking is necessary. One man was impotent because of his wife's fear of being overheard by neighbors through the paper-thin walls of their retirement apartment. But the problem was easily solved. On the spur of the moment they simply moved their bed to the other side of the room and away from the neighbor's wall—creative thinking!

Another case involved a man who worried unnecessarily because only one of his testicles was descended. Because of a low sperm count, he felt like "half a man." New intimacy developed when he and his wife began to speak the truth in love. He told his wife, a nurse, to stop acting like a nurse in bed. She told him, an auto mechanic, to stop tinkering with the mechanics of it all. Because they had a loving marriage, their intuitive confrontations were successful. They creatively worked out their problems.

Creative, intuitive thinking comes from the right brain, a nonverbal source of wisdom. More diffuse than the left brain, the right intuits meanings and new patterns. Perhaps the site of cosmic consciousness, this part of the brain is able to grasp seemingly irrelevant bits and pieces and put them together in a new pattern. To use the mind logically and creatively, both sides of the cerebral cortex need to be engaged. Many couples need to give themselves "permission" to think in new ways.

In developing greater sexual intimacy, a couple needs to do more than increase their sensory awareness and improve their thinking abilities. They also need to take into consideration the traditions, prejudices, and training that each of them has.

Traditions and prejudices

One well-known story of tradition is of a South Seas island people. They were relatively free of prejudices about sexual positions and didn't feel there was one way it *ought* to be done. Then the missionaries came along and taught that there was only one right way to have intercourse, with the man on top of the woman. Since then it's been humorously known as the missionary position, although many other positions provide as much or more satisfaction.

I remember that, when I was a little girl, my parents, with locked bedroom door, slept in late on Sunday mornings. Only I knew they weren't sleeping, as I could sometimes hear them talking and giggling. I used to wonder about the giggling as it seemed to be the only time and place they were like that. Did that become part of my tradition? Perhaps so. I do like long, loving Sunday mornings. In fact when the children were little, I used to put orange juice and graham crackers by their beds Saturday nights so that they would be happy if they awakened earlier than we wanted.[12]

Many cultural and family traditions have taught that sexual pleasure should not be affirmed, only denied. Or pleasure affirmed only by men, not by women. Some people rebel against these restrictive traditions and go to the other extreme. They need to remember, however, that external rebellion is not the same as internal freedom.[13]

One couple who were learning about their physical and emotional needs were able to express their shared sexual values this way: "Orgasm is always great but, if necessary, we can do without it. We don't need it the same way we need food or sleep. Also, having kids is great, but if we don't we can still have a loving marriage. The truth is, in fact, that what we need most is intimacy. Our ultimate goal of intercourse is not going to be just orgasm or reproduction—great as both are. Our goal is going to be learning how to love."

Learning how to love requires body, mind, and spirit. The mind may be alert or quiet, the emotions high or at rest, the body energized or fatigued. Regardless of the state of mind, body, and spirit, a person who is loving knows what it means to feel like a real, live person—a psychologically healthy person. Abraham Maslow describes this person:

> *Generally speaking, the psychologically healthy individual seems more likely to form a strong, happy, lasting marriage. It is not a selfless marriage, but rather a healthily selfish marriage in which each partner enjoys the other and the other's success. Although they take great pleasure in each other's company, they are capable of standing long separation or death philosophically. Each partner in a healthy marriage increases the confidence and self-respect of the other, they are good for each other.*[14]

Learning how to love leads to happiness. Happiness is a sense of well-being. Learning to love is not easy, yet love with intimacy and affirmation is a creative power that can unite two separate people and still allow for their separateness.

Chapter 8

"What are you doing down there?"

"I'm just sitting on the floor reading a book."

"But why behind a chair?"

"Because that's where I found the book."

"That's odd. Why not sit in the chair?"

"Because right now it feels good on the floor, down here where I'm reading."

"Would you mind stopping to talk to me for a moment?"

"Of course not. I'll even sit in the chair now."

"You're funny, and I love you."

"You're not funny, and I love you, too."

You and Your Marriage: The Present

Sometimes it's difficult to know where people are. They may seem to be present, but they're not. Their bodies are in one place—in fantasy they're somewhere else. The "somewhere else" may be many miles away and far into the future, or close by, yet deep into the past.

Here and now

The present is always related to the past. Your marriage is what it is *today* largely because of the past. The things that happened to you, the decisions you made—way back then—are part of the present.

The present is also related to the future. What your marriage is *now* is partly related to your future goals. For example, both of you may want an extended vacation and be saving your money for it *now*. One of you may want a career change and be studying for it *now*, or you may want more flowers in your garden and be planting seeds *now*.

Saving money *now* may mean simpler meals, fewer movies, postponing desired purchases for vacation pleasure in the future. Studying *now* may mean less time to be with your friends, less time to go hiking, less time for hobbies—all this now for a new job later. Planting seeds *now* may mean a sore back, tired muscles, grimy hands *now*.

While recognizing the importance of past and future, couples need to focus on the present—the here and now. Recently one wife complained, "Even though we sit across the table from each other, we don't seem to be *present* to each other. I always seem to be going over the past in my mind; he always seems to be involved in what's going to happen next week or next month on his job. Why aren't we *here* for each other *now* instead of being here in body but not in spirit?"

Understanding the space concept of "here" and the time concept of "now" is very important in any marriage. The exercises in this chapter are designed to help you evaluate your present situation, its strengths and weaknesses. They will help you recognize (1) the needs you and your partner have, (2) your problems and how to solve them, and (3) how to increase the four kinds of intimacy in your marriage. The parts of TA theory and application that will be integrated into this chapter are strokes, transactions, and time structuring.

Facing up to the present of your marriage takes courage and it's not easy. But you can decide to enjoy your marriage—here and now. This chapter will show you how.

Order, Security, and Freedom

Each person has basic needs that he or she strives to meet, either as a separate person or in the context of the marriage. Consider the needs in your marriage, and how these needs show (or how they are hidden).

Description of my needs	*Description of partner's needs*
For order in marriage	For order in marriage
For security in marriage	For security in marriage
For freedom in marriage	For freedom in marriage

If you and your partner have similar needs, your marriage has important areas in which you are compatible.

If your needs are conflicting, that is, you want more order and your partner wants more freedom, both of you may experience considerable tension. If so, what do you do with your tension?

Risk and the Courage to Be

To risk is to courageously take a chance. The chance is to maybe win, maybe lose. If partners are fairly certain they will win by acting in a particular way, they seldom need to gather up their courage to do so. If they are less sure, or if they feel a great deal is at stake, they need courage. Consider your patterns.

A risk I'm taking now

Possible results of risking

A risk I wouldn't take now

Possible results of not risking

Property and Privacy

In many traditional marriages husbands are expected to make the "big" decisions about things such as buying insurance, investing in property, or purchasing a car. Many wives make the decisions about things that are less expensive, such as a new set of dishes or clothes for the children.

Decisions about property can be major sources of conflict in any marriage, as can decisions about privacy. These are sometimes made by mutual agreement, sometimes not.

Things I need just for myself

Things my partner needs

Things we need together

Privacies I need

Privacies my partner needs

Privacies we need from the rest of the world

When there is a difference of opinion about property or privacy, what do you do about it?

Honor, Equality, and Truth

This exercise is an exercise in truth. Be especially truthful with yourself as you work this through.

I honor my spouse for	*How the honor shows*	*My spouse honors me for*	*How the honor shows*
______________	______________	______________	______________
______________	______________	______________	______________
______________	______________	______________	______________

How we're equal	*How our equality shows*	*How we're unequal*	*How this affects our marriage*
______________	______________	______________	______________
______________	______________	______________	______________
______________	______________	______________	______________

Subjects we are truthful about	*Subjects we avoid talking about*	*Subjects we are not truthful about*	*How this affects our marriage*
______________	______________	______________	______________
______________	______________	______________	______________
______________	______________	______________	______________

Can you see a pattern in the above areas that shows where and when needs are being met and where and when they are not?

Commitment and Responsibility

When people speak of commitment, they define it with phrases such as "a pledge to do something" or being "emotionally involved" or "intellectually bound."

When they speak of responsibility, they often speak of a burden or duty—either legal or ethical. So the two words, though seemingly similar, are different.

How would you define your commitment to your marriage? Do you experience it yourself? How does it show? Is your partner committed? How does it show?

How about responsibilities in your marriage? Are they defined as "shoulds" or "musts" or "ought to's"? Do they feel like burdens? How might your partner respond to these questions?

Problems: Here and Now

The major causes of divorce or physical or emotional separation are unsolved problems. Many partners believe some problems are unimportant or that change is impossible, so why try. Or they leave it to the other person to solve the problem.

> List your here-and-now problems (boredom, sex, money, in-laws, and so forth) and tell what you're doing or not doing about them.

Problems we try to ignore

Problems we procrastinate on

Problems we're working on

Now consider the small problems. Is there any chance they might grow bigger and become major problems or catastrophes?

Now, the ones you're procrastinating about, how might they get better or worse?

Our Problem-Solving Techniques

The fact that you are reading this book means that you already have some problem-solving skills and are looking for more.

Consider your strengths and weaknesses:

My strengths are

My weaknesses are

Kinds of problems I usually solve are

Kinds of problems that are hard for me to solve are

Consider your partner's skills in problem solving:

My partner's strengths are

My partner's weaknesses are

Problems my partner can usually solve are

Problems hard for my partner to solve are

As you look over the above, what are the implications for your marriage at the present time?

Sex Rating Scale

Many of the problems that occur in marriage are due to partners' lack of information on this topic. The following exercise from George Bach's *The Intimate Enemy* is to help you become aware of touch preferences.[1]

	Self (What I like)	*Other (What I think my partner likes)*
1. *Gentle throughout.* I never like to be handled aggressively.		
2. *Primarily gentle.* I like things to become occasionally, but very briefly, aggressive.		
3. *Aggressive gentle.* I like things mixed, as momentary mood dictates, but never anything as in 6 and 7 below.		
4. *Genitally aggressive.* I like to be firmly handled in sex, but without extra aggression.		
5. *Aggressive.* I like to be very firmly and very aggressively handled in sex but not hurt or threatened.		
6. *Threatened violent aggressive.* I like to be threatened with physical attacks.		
7. *Violent aggressive.* I like to be physically hurt in sex: bitten or pinched, or pinned down or hurtfully slapped, squeezed, and so on. This turns me on and makes me more passionate.		

Now plan for some uninterrupted time and discuss the exercise with your partner. Think about what it means for you personally to have the touch preferences you have.

The Four Forms of Intimacy

The essence of intimacy is closeness, warmth, trust, and openness. The human desire for intimacy is often thwarted because of hurtful experiences or repressive training in childhood, or because it is given a low priority in marriage. Yet the need for intimacy is universal; we all have the urge to experience it.

Evaluate intimacies in your marriage.

Times when I feel an intimacy of values *are*

Factors that encourage this feeling seem to be

Times when I feel intellectual intimacy *are*

Factors that encourage this feeling seem to be

Times when I feel emotional intimacy *are*

The factors that encourage this feeling seem to be

Times when I feel sexual intimacy *are*

Factors that encourage this feeling seem to be

If you and your spouse are satisfied with your level of intimacy, rejoice! If not, begin to think about what you would each need to do differently.

Increasing Intimacy

This exercise requires the commitment of both you and your partner. As you first learn how to do it, try doing it on a twice-a-week basis. Each session requires fifteen minutes of quiet, uninterrupted clock time. The details are important.

Put two straight chairs very close together, facing each other. Sit in them so that your eyes are no more than thirty inches apart.

Agree not to look away from each other—not up, down, or sideways—during the entire fifteen minutes.

Agree to talk to each other and not be silent or use rituals, pastimes, or games to avoid intimacy.

Talk about anything you like, according to the above rules. Remember to keep looking at each other. Now evaluate your intimacy level.

What kind of intimacy was involved? What are your criteria for judging?

Target stroking for a loving marriage

The word *stroke* is an important Transactional Analysis word that refers to any kind of recognition. The recognition can be verbal, such as, "Hello, honey, I'm glad you're home." It can be nonverbal, such as a wink or sexy gesture that conveys the message, "I see you and I want you."

Strokes can also be conditional or unconditional. Most strokes given in marriage are conditional, tied in with promises for the future. They may not be verbalized, but the true message might be "If you help me clean up the kitchen I might get sexy tonight," or "If you come right home after work, I might fix you a good dinner." The message is easily conveyed with facial expression or tone of voice. Unconditional strokes are given in situations of close intimacy. The message behind these strokes—whether verbalized or not—is "I love you for who you are, not just for what you do."

Strokes can also be positive or negative. "Spaghetti again (with a frown)," "Late again (with a sneer)," "You never do anything around here (with a whiny tone of voice)," and "How come you never take me out (with a pout)" are all negative strokes. They are given to make the partner feel bad in some way.

Frequently, the bad feelings one partner wants the other to experience are feelings of guilt, shame, or inadequacy. Sometimes these strokes are so painful they are felt as a stab in the back or kick in the groin. They "hit the target" in a very negative way and are destructive, even sadistic.

Positive strokes are very different. They create excitement and warmth and closeness between two people. They are compliments, pleasurable touches, gifts, or acts of acceptance.

Some partners withhold positive strokes by withdrawing physically or emotionally. They may go to the garage or some other space "to be alone." They may be very resentful and have a higher investment in staying resentful than in solving problems. Verbally, or nonverbally one may blame the other, complain about the other, abstain from getting close to the other.

Target stroking is stroking that gives the person just what he or she wants. Positive target stroking is a learned skill that anyone can acquire. Sometimes the first step is letting go of past resentments and *deciding to live this marriage in the present time*—here and now—and to be gracious and glad for the positive things that can be experienced.

Sometimes the first step is to stop, look, and listen. Listening to your partner takes time. Looking—really looking at your partner—takes a decision. The decision might be to stop fantasizing about someone else, or to stop being a workaholic, or to stop procrastinating and do something.

Turning on the senses can be another first step. Becoming aware and using all the senses, especially intuition, usually brings people into the present, out of the past and out of the future. In the present, people can ask themselves, "What is going on *here and now* that I can express appreciation for?" "How shall I show my appreciation?" "What would be a positive target stroke that I could give?"

The effects of positive target stroking can be observed. A partner's eyes will light up. He or she will become more lively, often more sexy, often more able to solve problems.[2]

Childhood Strokes and Marriage Now

In childhood all people learn about strokes. Some discover they can't have as many as they want, or they can't have the kind they want. They may try harder and harder to get them. Other people, feeling hopeless, stop asking for strokes and may also stop giving them to others. This exercise is to show you how childhood experiences with stroking are often continued into the present. Let your memory drift back to childhood and recall the forms of recognition you received.

Strokes I received in childhood that were related to my needs for order, security, risk, and so forth were

Strokes I currently get that are similar or different are

Strokes I received about my sexuality were

Strokes I currently get that are similar or different are

Strokes I received about my problem-solving skills were

Strokes I currently get that are similar or different are

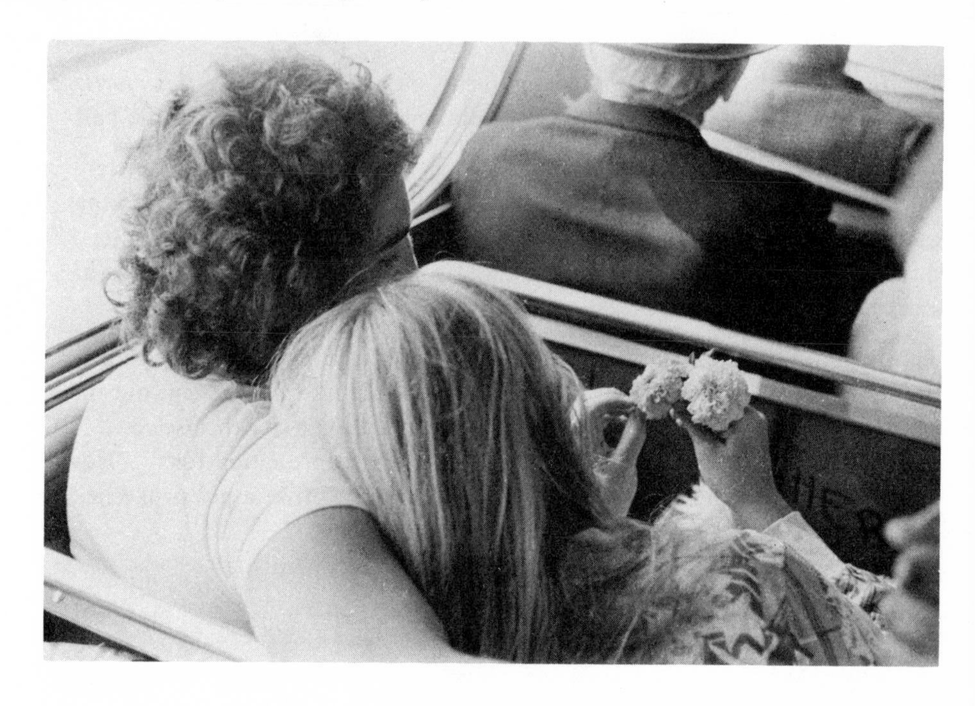

Stroke Assessment

For this exercise, define the word *now* as the last twenty-four hours. Then record the strokes given and received between you and your partner.

Strokes I gave		*Strokes my partner gave*	
Verbal	*Nonverbal*	*Verbal*	*Nonverbal*
________	________	________	________
________	________	________	________
________	________	________	________
Positive	*Negative*	*Positive*	*Negative*
________	________	________	________
________	________	________	________
________	________	________	________

Conditional	*Unconditional*	*Conditional*	*Unconditional*
______________	______________	______________	______________
______________	______________	______________	______________
______________	______________	______________	______________

Now consider, which strokes were well received?

Which were ignored or rejected?

Can you see a stroke pattern in your marriage?

Is your relationship loving?

Target Strokes and Ego States

Each ego state needs specific strokes. The Parent in one person might feel target stroked by regular church attendance. In another person, the stroke to the Parent ego state might be a perfectly clean house. The Adult ego state deserves strokes for thinking logically. It also needs stroking for acting on the basis of objective data. The Child wants unconditional strokes just for being alive. It also needs strokes for performance. Now fill in the blanks.

When I stroke my partner positively by ____________________________,

I intend the stroke to go to the ____________________________ego state.

My partner responds to my stroke by ____________________________.

Was or was not ____________ the stroke received as I intended?

When the stroke is received it seems to hit the target in my partner's

________________________ego state.

When the stroke is not received or is received negatively, it means you've missed the target.

If you think more awareness will enhance your marriage, keep a twenty-four-hour diary.

Have you told your spouse what your target strokes are?

Touching Strokes

Any kind of touch is a stroke. Some kind of touching, like being held too tightly, or having sex without lubrication, is painful and negative. Some touches, like being held close when grief-stricken, or being caressed gently before sex, are pleasurable and positive. You can become more aware of the touch patterns in your marriage by recalling the past forty-eight hours.

How did you initiate touching? What kind?

When? Where? How often?

What response did you get? Was it what you expected?

How did your spouse initiate touching? What kind?

When? Where? How often?

What response did you give? Was it an expected response?

Are the above touch patterns typical in your marriage?

Think of one touch pattern that needs to be improved. What is it you do now? What do you want to do?

Fantasize yourself doing what you want to do. See yourself touching and being touched in new ways. Plan to do it in the next twenty-four hours.

Courage and Strokes

It often takes courage to change stroking patterns. Because partners may not feel courageous, they do not act to change the patterns. Acting courageously is a here-and-now step to a more satisfying marriage. *Courage is acting positively in spite of internal fear.*

This exercise will help you discover that many of your fears may be unrealistic. They are left over from the past and do not really exist in the present. Fill in the following and discover new courage:

One stroke I really want from my partner is

I don't ask for it because I'm afraid that

The worst thing that could happen if my fear is actualized is

After that, the worst thing that could happen is

And then the worst thing is

Therefore, is the stroke I want worth asking for?

If I decide *not* to ask I will feel

If I *do* ask I will feel

Transactions in marriage

In TA terms, the things that people do and say to each other are called transactions. In a transaction, each person gains something from the exchange. What they give and what they get depend upon which ego state in each person is most active at the time and the kinds of transactions that go on between them.

In every transaction, there is at least one stimulus, which is a stroke of some kind, and one response, also a stroke. "Hi, Harriet" is a positive stimulus stroke. "Hi, Bill, how are you?" is a positive response stroke. Together, the two strokes make up a *complementary* transaction.

If the response to a stimulus is not an expected one, the transaction is said to be *crossed.* This occurs if the greeting, "Hi, Harriet," gets a critical response such as "Don't you see I'm busy?" or a plaintive response such as "Please don't ask me how I am." With such responses, Bill is likely to feel crossed up somehow.

The third type of transaction is *ulterior.* It is called this because an ostensible Adult-to-Adult stimulus partially hides a different message that is directed to the Child ego state in the other person. A "Hi, Harriet" given with a wink or a sneer is the first part of an ulterior transaction. The ulterior message is usually given by body language or tone of voice.

Complementary transactions

A complementary transaction occurs when a person gets the expected response from the other person. It can occur between any two ego states. Complementary transactions, diagramed with parallel lines, fit into the following patterns in many marriages:

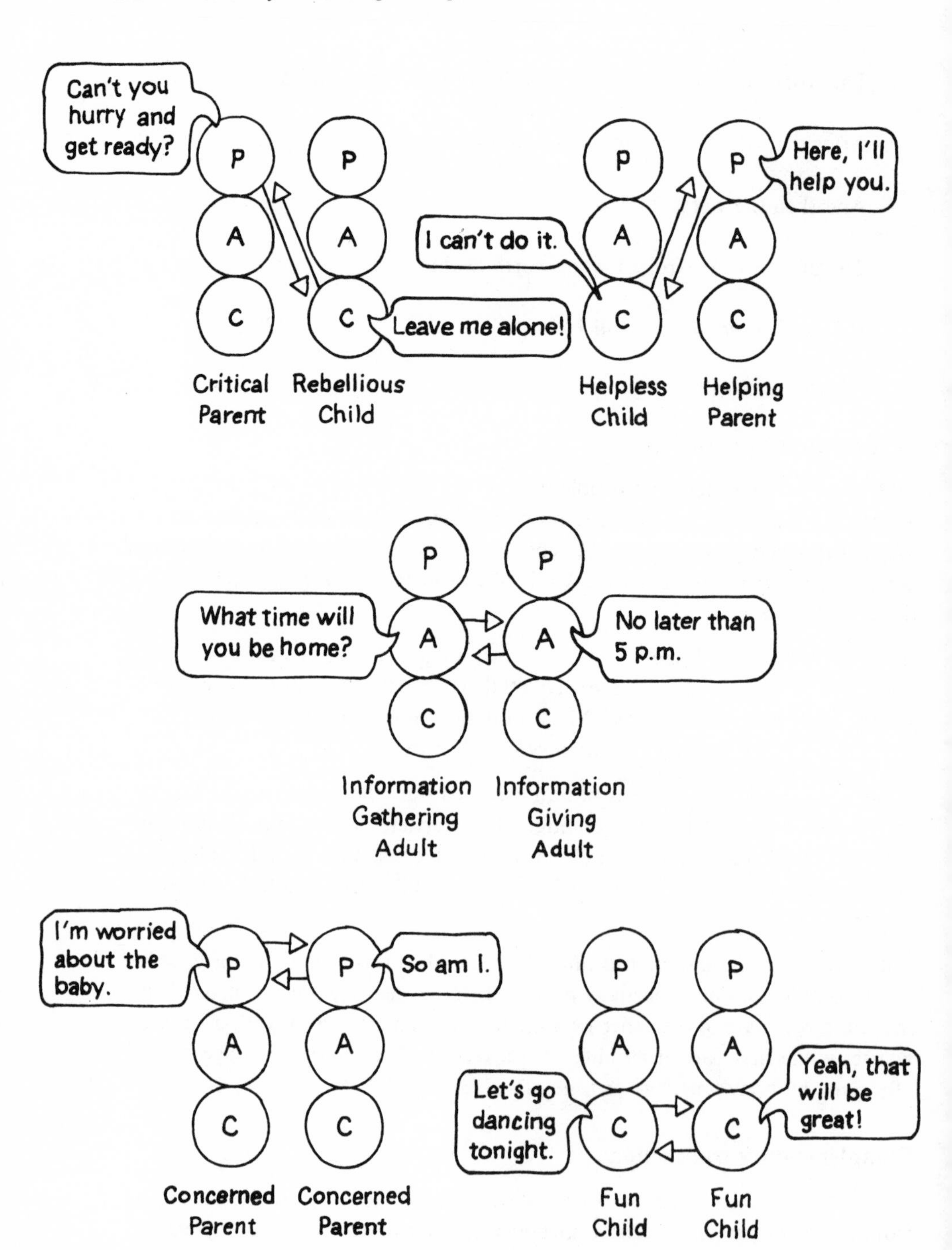
Can't you hurry and get ready?
P
A
C
P
A
C
Leave me alone!
Critical Parent
Rebellious Child
I can't do it.
P
A
C
P
A
C
Here, I'll help you.
Helpless Child
Helping Parent
What time will you be home?
P
A
C
P
A
C
No later than 5 p.m.
Information Gathering Adult
Information Giving Adult
I'm worried about the baby.
P
A
C
P
A
C
So am I.
Concerned Parent
Concerned Parent
Let's go dancing tonight.
P
A
C
P
A
C
Yeah, that will be great!
Fun Child
Fun Child

In any marriage, many transactions are complementary and routine. Constant complementary transactions are not always good, however. For example, if two people continually have Parent-to-Child complementary transactions, then they can become locked into specific roles. Or a routine of complementary transactions can become boring, and a couple may break away from each other or have a fight. When they do either of these things, it's because they want their marriage to be more dynamic.

Some people prefer routine marriages that are orderly, predictable, and therefore safe. Others prefer dynamic marriages in which each person is fluid, changing, and growing. These people are free to switch ego states and do not limit themselves to complementary transactions. Consequently, they don't feel stuck or bored with each other.

Crossed transactions and conflicts

In a routine-type marriage without risk, courage, and freedom, couples often begin to feel bored, resentful, or "stuck" with each other. Routine marriages often overuse one particular kind of complementary transaction, such as critical Parent to inadequate Child, or nurturing Parent to angry Child. Eventually this leads to complaints: "We always seem to do the same old things. Nothing new ever happens to us." Perhaps you've felt that way at times in your marriage.

Conflict is possible whenever a crossed transaction interrupts the familiar pattern. "Hey, you're not acting normal! What's the matter with you, anyhow?" or, "You've got the problem, not me, so what are you going to do about it?"

Sometimes these accusations are enough to make a person pack up and leave. Or the partners stay and begin to use a series of crossed transactions. They may hope to clarify a problem, or make a decision, or improve their marriage at the present time—or they may hope to make their partner feel bad.

The process from a routine marriage, to conflict, to resolution or withdrawal has several steps:

Routine marriage ⟶ Feeling bored ⟶ Wanting excitement ⟶
Crossed transactions ⟶ Conflict emerges ⟶
Resolution or withdrawal

There are four common types of crossed transactions. They can be diagramed with dialogue that shows unmet needs.

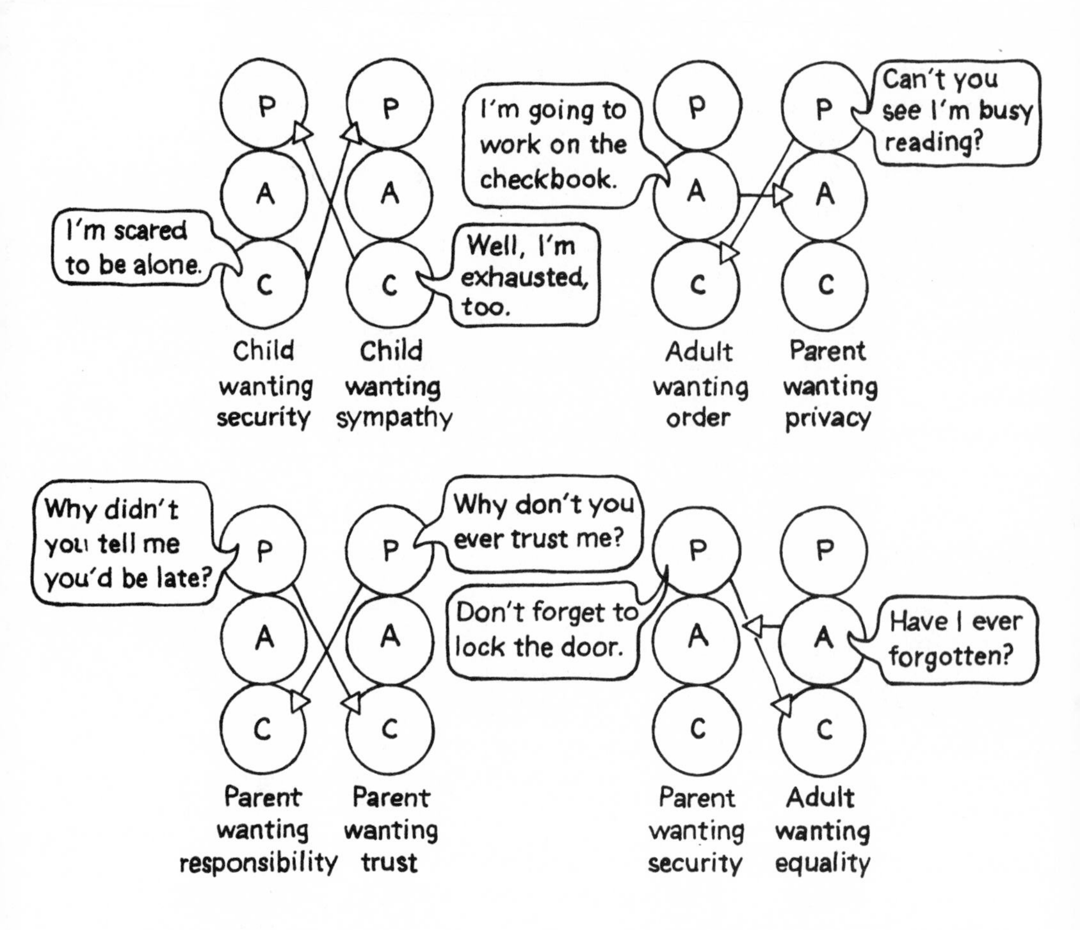

Crossed transactions are unavoidable in most interpersonal relationships. So are conflicts. Learning how and why cross-ups occur and sometimes lead to conflict is crucial in every marriage. It's also crucial to learn how to use and cope with these kinds of transactions.

They occur when one person "crosses" what the other person intended to be a complementary transaction. They often indicate conflicts in needs or values. Many people become anxious or angry when they are crossed or cross others, or when they are faced with conflict. Thus cross-ups can destroy a relationship; sometimes, however, they can help it grow.

Cross-ups can be ignored, escalated, or "worked through." When worked through, problems are usually resolved in positive rather than negative ways. It usually takes courage to undo cross-ups. It also takes planning and creativity.

Ulterior transactions

Ulterior transactions have a hidden agenda. They are more complex than complementary and crossed transactions because they involve more than two ego states at once. The way it works it that while two ego states exchange a spoken message, other ego states are sending a different, "psychological" message.

The actual words that are spoken are called the social transaction. In diagrams, they are indicated by a solid arrow. The ulterior message, or psychological transaction, is diagramed with a dotted arrow. Common ulterior transactions in a marriage are shown here in diagram form.

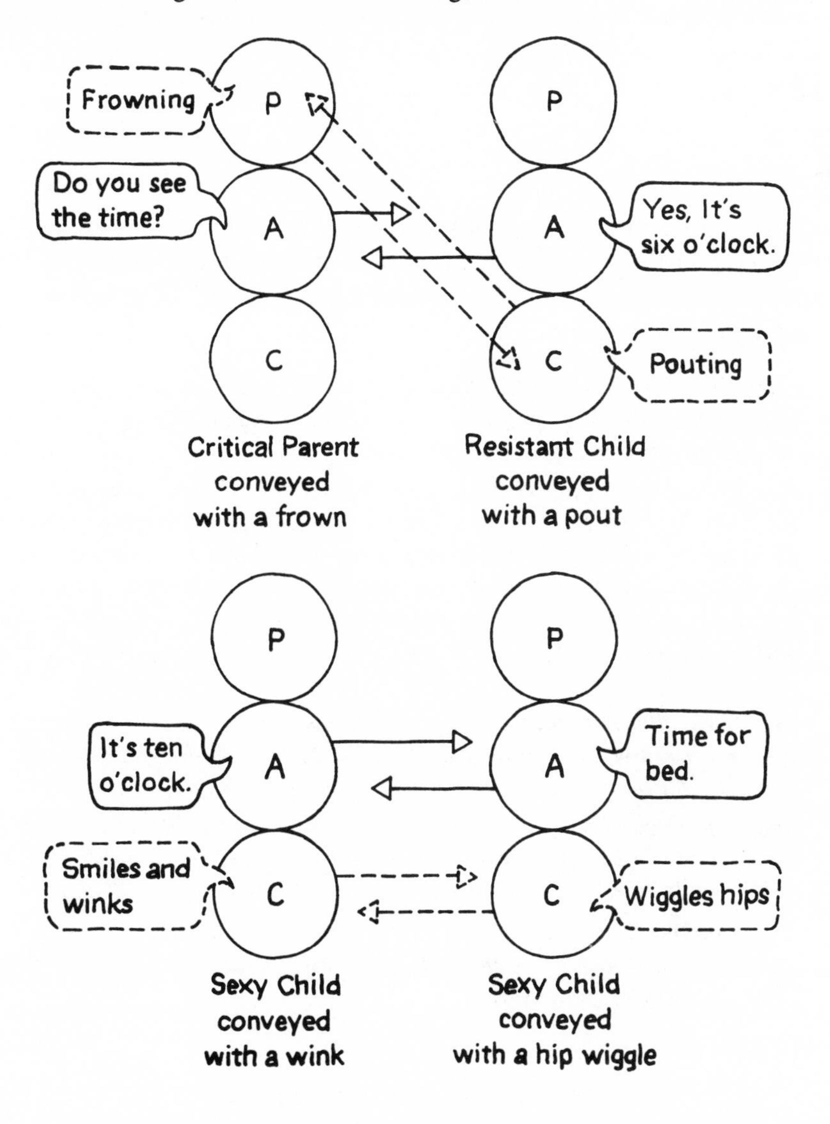

At the social level, the Adult ego state in the diagrams seems to be doing the talking. Actually, it is one of the other ego states that is sending the "psychological" message.

The ulterior message is often given by body language, facial expression, or tone of voice. A husband may, for example, angrily pound a kitchen table, turn away abruptly, or give an encouraging pat on the shoulder. Or consider the ulterior message when a wife winks seductively, laughs joyfully, or frowns disapprovingly. A husband who plaintively whines, uses a sarcastic tone of voice, or looks helplessly confused conveys a powerful message.

The creative ability, present in every Child ego state, is often used to send out ulterior messages. It is the intuitive ability, which everyone also has in the Child ego state, that is used to pick up ulterior messages.

Games people play

A psychological game is a series of transactions in which one or more players ends up feeling *not* OK. Games are learned in childhood, and people are seldom aware that they play them. Ulterior transactions are basic moves in any game. As described in the book *A New Self:*

> *Everyone plays psychological games at times. Like solitaire, games can be played singly; like chess, they can be two-handed; like basketball, a number of players may be involved.*
>
> *In every case, the players have some "under the surface" awareness of the rules and choose to play, often because they don't know any better. Most people are trained not to ask directly for what they want or need from others. So, some hint at their needs by looking sad and acting helpless, or by stamping their feet and acting angry, or by smiling hopefully and acting encouragingly. Others get what they want by verbally manipulating those around them.*
>
> *People usually manipulate others not because they want to, but because they don't know what to do instead. Or, they are afraid their direct requests will be ignored, ridiculed, or punished in some way.*
>
> *People play psychological games because they learn to do so in childhood. It feels safer to be evasive and indirect about one's needs than to risk the rejection that could follow a straightforward request.*
>
> *The common dramatic roles—Victim, Persecutor, and Rescuer—are played out as minidramas in each game, with players usually switching roles as the game progesses.*

At the end of a game, one or more of the players involved collects negative feelings, such as anger, depression, confusion, or hurt. Sometimes a game player collects a self-righteous feeling, feels blameless, and accuses others of playing games.[3]

Cross-ups in Your Marriage

Cross-ups occur when one person gives an unexpected response or responds from an ego state that is not expected to be active.

In the two diagrams here, add your own dialogue and the lines from one ego state to another. Focus on value collisions.

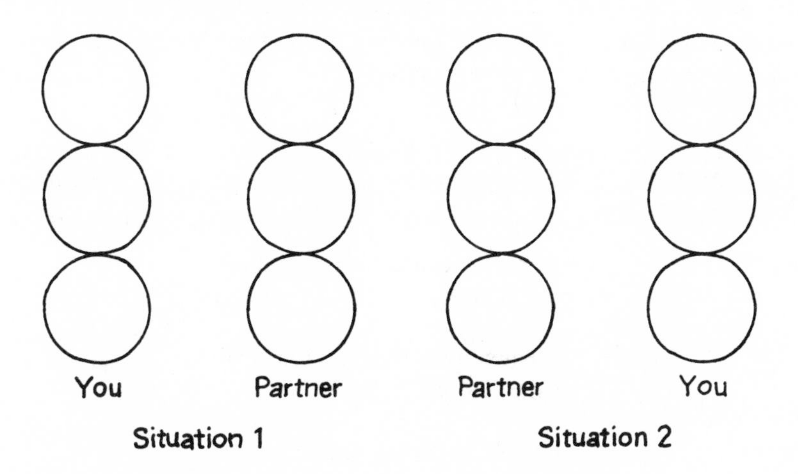

What are other options the two of you might have used?

From Routine to Dynamic Marriage

The purpose of this exercise is to help you get in touch with the convenient parts of routine and the exciting parts of nonroutine.

The routines in marriage (same food, same friends, same sex position) are the static, nonchanging ways of transacting. The dynamics in marriage are the changing, growing, new ways of transacting (new menus, new friends, new experiments in sex). Dynamic changes, like routines can be either positive or negative.

Negative routines in our marriage

Positive routines in our marriage

Negative dynamics in our marriage

Positive dynamics in our marriage

On a scale of 1 to 10 (with 10 being high), how dynamic is your marriage?

Games Couples Play

Couples often play games to avoid intimacy or because they haven't figured out what to do instead. Sometimes they are playing out life scripts. Games have names and themes. What are yours?

Name of game	*Theme of game*	*We play (don't play) this game*
Harried	Being "too busy" to complete things well.	
Kick Me	Frequently getting disapproval from people.	
Cornered	Unable to please someone, no matter what.	
I'm Only Trying to Help You	Continually being available to help others.	
Blemish	Nit-picking and frequently finding little things wrong.	
Now I've Got You, You S.O.B.	Waiting for people to make mistakes, then pouncing.	
Wooden Leg	Exploiting a misfortune to avoid responsibility.	
Debtor	Taking out more and more loans and credit cards.	

Now look at the games you play. How do the games affect your marriage?

Are your games related to your needs, views, or values?

The Game Plan

The Game Plan, designed by John James, is based on the idea that each game has a plan of action, much like the plans that football players use for their plays.[4] Each plan has a predictable pattern, as in the following example.

Sis:	(Asks a favor)
Pa:	"No."
Sis:	"Why not?"
Pa:	"Because, last time you . . . (put down). . . ."
Sis:	"Well, that's not true. . . ."
Pa and Sis:	(Argue loudly)
Sis:	(Leaves the room yelling)
Pa:	(Reads the paper)
Sis:	(Feels mad)
Pa:	(Feels mad)

To discover one of your game plans, write down answers to the following.

What keeps happening over and over that leaves one of you feeling bad?

How does it start?

What happens next?

How does it end?

How does each person feel when it ends?

A game can be broken up at any point by either of the persons involved if one of them decides to do something differently or feel differently than they normally would. What could each person have done differently that would have changed your game?

Time structuring in TA

According to TA, people structure their time with other people in six ways: psychological withdrawal, rituals, pastimes, games, activities, and intimacy. Actually, it is often during activities that the other forms of time structuring occur.

Two parties might be working together on a project (activity) and one or both might daydream about being somewhere else (psychological withdrawal). Or they might greet each other with stereotyped transactions (ritual), or chat informally about sports, family, and so forth (pastime), or get involved in an argument (often, though not always, a game), or experience closeness, openness, and trust (intimacy).

Each form of time structuring, except for game playing, can be used to enhance marriage. Or it can be abused and thus decrease the joy of life.

In loving marriages there is always a sense of basic trust and a willingness to be real and let the other person also be real. There is responsible caring without exploitation and manipulation. Neither acts as master or slave, as owner or object to be possessed.[5]

Withdrawal can be physical or emotional. People withdraw physically from others when they avoid a discussion and go for a walk alone or go into a room and close the door. Some withdraw emotionally by just pulling into their own heads, letting their minds go blank or engaging in fantasies of "What if I were with someone else?" or "If only I had a million dollars!" Withdrawal is negative when partners sulk and indulge themselves by wallowing in negative feelings of loneliness, self-pity, hostility, or resentment. It is positive when partners stop superficial chattering and start getting in touch with how they feel and what they need.

Rituals are stereotyped transactions that are highly predictable. Saying "Hello" and getting a "Hello" back is a two-stroke ritual. "How are you?" "Fine," is another two-stroke ritual. Many rituals are centered around family life, national traditions, holidays, religious beliefs, and so forth. Some of them add order and pleasant predictablility to people's lives; some hold deep meaning, such as certain religious rituals or the ritual of getting married. However, if a whole life is primarily patterned by ritualistic living, people's growth and development are inhibited because they don't risk new, creative ways of thinking, feeling, and behaving.

Pastiming, another common way of spending time, often follows a ritual greeting. In pastiming, people simply talk to one another about subjects that are of little consequence. One of the most common pastimes that people engage in is centered around the topic of the weather. "Gee, it sure is hot." "Yeah, summer's coming." Or "Gee, it sure is cold." "Maybe it's going to snow tonight." Any subject can be used as a pastime—cars, friends, current records, TV shows, and so forth. Pastimes are sometimes a waste of time. How often, for example, does something productive come out of an exchange about the weather? When weather affects an activity such as farming or sailing, then the discussion is more than just passing time.

Psychological games are always unproductive uses of time, since people play them solely to avoid doing something positive like solving a problem, making a decision, or getting close to other people.

Games result in bad feelings because people play games to get and give negative strokes, often without knowing it. Structuring time with games often indicates that the players are involved in feelings of the past or manipulative plans for the future. They are reinforcing their negative positions and feelings rather than getting involved in what's going on right now.

Activities are what is commonly called work—getting something done, getting something accomplished. People who work on a project together, who cook a meal or repair a car together, are involved in activities. Many daily activities are related to people's jobs, their education, or their hobbies.

Generally speaking, activities are useful and rewarding ways to spend time. However, a life that is exclusively made up of activities, especially solitary activities, may be somewhat sterile, devoid of social courtesies, friendly laughter, or lively sex. "All we do is work, work, work," partners might say to each other, "We don't seem to have time to play together and have fun."

Intimacy implies an open relationship with no ulterior transactions. It is game-free. During moments of intimacy people do not try to get anything out of each other. They are not possessive and jealous, or demanding and insisting. They are simply being with one another, listening to one another, and caring about one another. In intimate moments, people feel appreciative, warm, tender, affectionate. These feelings may be expressed through joyful laughter, or caring gestures, or peaceful silence, or interesting conversation, or passionate sex. Each of the four forms of intimacy has its unique way of being expressed.

Intimacy may be uncomfortable, particularly for people who have learned to be fearful and distrustful of others, to keep their distance, to avoid closeness. These people unknowingly choose games, rituals, or pastimes to avoid being "real" or too emotionally close to other people.

Many couples avoid intimacy because it involves risk. When intimate, both partners are vulnerable, so they may find it less threatening to withdraw psychologically, engage in pastimes, or play psychological games. Another risk of intimacy is that if marriage partners are open to each other, their needs, values, and views about marriage may be challenged. And challenge is often threatening. However, if the challenge is responded to, the marriage may grow and change for the better.

Overall, the activities couples share and the moments of intimacy they experience together are the most positive ways they can structure their time. Through activities and intimacy, they can get and give winning strokes.

Your Time Management

How do you and your spouse commonly use time when you are together on a weekend, or on a weekday? Focusing on the *present* use of time in your marriage, fill in blanks.

Use of time	*Typical weekday*	*Typical weekend*
Withdrawals	__________	__________
Rituals	__________	__________
Pastimes	__________	__________
Games	__________	__________
Activities	__________	__________
Intimacy	__________	__________

Intimacy often develops during some shared activity, or in prime time used to plan or review the activity. When do you and your partner feel intimate? If you rarely do, how do you avoid intimacy?

Sex and Time

Intercourse is closely associated with time. "We don't have time," is a common lament. "Let's take time," can be the response.

All six ways of structuring time can be part of sexual experience. For example, psychological withdrawal from a spouse into a fantasy of being with someone else is common, as are the sexual rituals many couples use. Sex may be merely a pastime when there doesn't seem to be much else to do, or a game of exploitation. Occasionally, it is an activity that seems to take a lot of work. And it is sometimes a series of acts that lead to close intimacy.

Use of time	*How we use our time sexually*	*What more is wanted*	*What less is wanted*
Withdrawal	__________	__________	__________
Ritual	__________	__________	__________

Pastimes	______	______	______
Games	______	______	______
Activities	______	______	______
Intimacy	______	______	______

The Time of Your Life

In the life of your marriage, there was a past when it was born. There will also be a future when it will live or die. *Now,* at the present time of your marriage, you probably experience several different kinds of time.

Clock-time experiences happen when

Challenging time experiences develop when

Prime-time experiences take place when

Leftover time occurs when

Out-of-time moments occur for us when

If your time is mostly by the clock, you may need to take a vacation for it. If so, how could you arrange it?

You and Your Space

This exercise will help you evaluate your private space, the space you share with your partner, and the time when you might be completely in that space or partially somewhere else.

My spaces	*How I use my spaces*	*How the time is structured*
______	______	______
______	______	______
______	______	______

Partner's spaces	*How the space is used*	*How the time is structured*
______	______	______
______	______	______
______	______	______

Our spaces	*How the space is used*	*How the time is structured*
______	______	______
______	______	______
______	______	______

As you review the above, are any improvements needed in allocation of space? use of space? time structuring in the space?

Loving Here, Loving Now

If you have read this far in this book, it probably means you either have a loving marriage or you intend to develop one.

Every need, every view, every value is important. All can be dealt with in loving ways or in nonloving ways. Evaluate your loving capacity when faced with problems.

Current problems that need solving in our marriage that seem related to our *needs* are

Loving problem-solving techniques could be

Current problems related to our *views* are

Loving problem-solving techniques could be

Current problems related to our *values* are

Loving problem-solving techniques could be

From present to future

All couples have needs and problems. For partners who want to get their needs met and solve their problems, quiet and solitude are often necessary. To find time alone, they may need to restructure the way they use their time. They certainly need motivation to change, courage to start doing it, and a plan that takes into account their time and energy. Loving marriages don't just happen, they are achievements of intimacy.

Couples who want happiness work toward increasing intimacy in all aspects of their marriages. They discover that they can have an *intimacy of values* as they meet crises that call for them to make important decisions about issues such as children, in-laws, and friends. They discover *intellectual intimacy,* which can develop with, for example, the open discussion of current events or personal values. They find out that it grows if both partners update their knowledge and increase their willingness to talk about—even argue about—the things that stimulate them intellectually.

These couples work for *emotional intimacy,* sharing feelings, dreams, and plans, sharing themselves, and giving and receiving love. They also know the *sexual intimacy* that comes with opening their senses, being in touch with their bodies, letting go of stereotyped or routine sexual behavior, and being willing to be "one," with and for the other person.

Part Three

If I had only . . .
forgotten future greatness
and looked at the green things and the buildings
and reached out to those around me
and smelled the air
and ignored the forms and the self-styled obligations
and heard the rain on the roof
and put my arms around my wife
. . . and it's not too late[1]

Hugh Prather

Marriage and the Future

Chapter 9

"What do you think we'll be doing in the year 2000?"

"I don't know—walking on the moon maybe? Or maybe the earth will have blown up by then."

"Well, probably we'll be grandparents, passing our evenings in rocking chairs on the porch."

"Do you really want to stay with me for that long? Do you think we'll ever make it to that porch?"

"I hope so. I really do. Anyway, I'm planning on it."

Hope for Future Loving

Many of you now reading this book will be alive and married in the year 2000. I hope to be. Will we be more fully human by that time, or will we be more oppressed by technology, nuclear war, greed, lust, overcrowding, and a decay of ethics?

It is 1978 as I write this. Since I'm sixty-one now, I'll be eighty-three then and eager to usher in the new century with fanfare and joy. To do that requires continual planning. Science fiction writers, philosophers, economists, and others from almost every field of human endeavor visualize the effects of cybernation, automation, hedonism, and so forth. Like unheard prophets of the past, many of them plead with us to recognize the possible disastrous consequences of future shock—the fragmentation that will affect each of us as a result of fast-paced technology that threatens our traditions, our values, and even our lives. It's a pessimistic view of the future and, unfortunately, one that may come true.

A remarkable book, Alvin Toffler's *Future Shock,* shows how the technological culture has created a continuing barrage of new inventions and situations so that many people tend to feel and act fragmented. Without a sense of continuity and roots, many more will experience physical and emotional distress, even breakdowns. They may lose their sense of identity if their traditional lifestyles, which once met the need for order and security, fade. Strongly held values will be challenged and, according to Toffler, little in life will be stable.

Six styles for the future

What about marriage in the future? Will it survive as a social custom? If so, what forms will it take?

We can only guess at the future, but at this time six types of marriage look as if they will persist. These are marriages that are (1) traditional, (2) directed by personal interest, (3) influenced by institutions, (4) nondirected, (5) group or communal, and (6) holistic.

Traditional marriage is likely to continue into the future. More firmly grounded in the past than any other form of marriage, its tradition comes from cultural patterns developed through the family. Basically, traditional marriages are experienced as "This is the way marriage *ought* to be, and other options are not as good."

"Yes," said Edna, "I'm going to get married in a white wedding gown and we're going to Niagara Falls for our honeymoon and then settle down and have three kids just like Mom and Dad."

Marriages for convenience, or for *personal interest,* will also continue into the future. The reasons for the convenience will probably remain the same as always—financial gain, a sexual partner, opportunities for prestige, and so forth. These are "trade-off" marriages, where each partner fills specific needs of the other. Many people assume that "May-December romances," in which one partner is much older than the other, are marriages of convenience. The younger partner may desire the support provided by a substitute parent; the older one may desire the physical and emotional excitement that youth can bring.

A growing number of marriages in the future will be *influenced by institutions.* Already this is happening in many parts of the world—planned marriages in the Soviet Union, planned families in China and India. Tax laws, welfare regulations, and social security laws often influence the decision of whether or not to marry in the United States. Religious organizations also strongly influence marriages and family planning. As some nations become stronger and more centralized, their control over marriages will undoubtedly increase.

The *nondirected marriage* is a product of the fast-paced "anything goes" mentality that has become a part of our culture. Joyce and David grew up in a time when acting "cool" and uninvolved was the ideal. They prided themselves on "not getting upset," and "living for today." They got married, they said, because "it felt right, and besides, if it doesn't work out, we can always get a divorce."

Most of these couples refuse to look at the future; they think that making commitments is a waste of time because the world might blow up tomorrow. This attitude is captured in Fritz Perls' words:

> *I do my thing, and you do your thing.*
> *I am not in this world to live up to your expectations,*
> *and you are not in this world to live up to mine.*
> *You are you, and I am I;*
> *If by chance we find each other, it's beautiful.*
> *If not, it can't be helped.*[1]

Personally, I don't believe situations "can't be helped." And I doubt whether Fritz totally believed what he said, even though some part of him gave up in hopelessness.[2]

The future will probably also bring more *group marriages* or communal living arrangements. Various people have experimented with group marriage since the time of Julius Caesar, who noted how common they were in the Northern

European tribes he conquered. The 1960s saw a renewed interest in group living, but most of these experiments didn't work out. Sometimes a group collapsed because it lacked an overall structure or sense of purpose. Other times the sexual gymnastics of switching partners became too much emotionally for everyone to handle.

Despite negative experiences with group living, some new urban and professional communes are forming that may point the way for groups in the future. Many of them are formed for a purpose: for religious study, to support each other professionally, and so forth. Members are often married and want to stay that way, so sexual promiscuity is not an issue. These groups sometimes provide a strong and loving community in which to raise children.

Holistic marriages are the hope of the future. In a holistic relationship, the individuals interact so as to become more than just two individuals. Holistic marriages encourage each partner to grow individually while both partners grow in love and unity. Couples in holistic marriages can look at and understand their past and free themselves from unproductive guilt and juvenile fantasies. At the same time they have the courage to face the present, to recognize their needs and to look at their problems honestly and solve them. They believe in their marriage, and they don't give up easily. They hope for the future because they find meaning in their love for each other.

The idea of a holistic marriage may be difficult to understand because most of us think of marriage as a dependent relationship rather than one of interdependence. This view of a relationship often comes from childhood.

Stages in marriage

Infants and young children *need to depend* on their parents. Adolescents tend to struggle for identity, rejecting advice and directions from authority figures. They *rebel against feeling dependent.* The next step for most young people is when they move away from home, become self-supporting, thinking and deciding for themselves, *becoming independent.* At a later point in life the now-grown children and their parents often develop a new relationship with mutual respect, caring, and love. They have become *interdependent by choice.*

Many couples go through similar stages. At first they may be overly dependent on each other, afraid of becoming individuals. If they cling to each other constantly, this creates future problems. As one husband complained, "I can't stand it. Everytime we go to a party she hangs on me like glue."

Some couples are caught up in a power struggle and fight each other as though they were still teenagers fighting against authority figures. Each wants power over the other and may try to get it with threats of leaving home or with statements that provoke more anger in the partner. "Don't tell me what to do! I'll do what I want, when I want."

Some couples reach an independent stage of "You go your way and I'll go mine." They live together only because it's convenient in some way.

Other couples may work together harmoniously and enjoy each other's company. They have found something more. The "something more" is an interdependence that is freely chosen and tenderly nurtured. Interdependence does not develop by happenstance; both partners need to work at it. Fortunately, the seeds for its growth exist in every relationship.

Interdependence often is a sign that a couple has developed a "third self." A third self is more than a combination of the two selves of the spouses. It is a new form that happens in marriages that are for loving, and it can be understood with simple mathematical formulas.

Mathematics of marriage

Imagine for a moment, a kind of "relationship mathematics," which Louis Savary and I first introduced in our book, *The Heart of Friendship.* These mathematical formulas can also be used to describe and understand four basic attitudes found in marriages.

The *first attitude* is expressed when both *partners feel incomplete* (only half-persons) unless, like Romeo and Juliet, they are united with each other. This is the typically romantic view of marriage.

It can also happen in a marriage of convenience where each partner fills the specific needs of the other. If both partners have this attitude, they are not really individuals, only half-people. They seem to lose their individual identities, like hydrogen and oxygen when combining to form water, and often are very possessive.

Mathematically, this marriage can be represented by the formula

$$\tfrac{1}{2}\text{ person} + \tfrac{1}{2}\text{ person} \longrightarrow 1\text{ person.}$$

The *second relating attitude* happens when *one person feels whole and independent but the other feels incomplete and dependent* (only half a person.) This too involves possessiveness. In this kind of marriage, one partner may act like a competent Adult or nurturing or critical Parent and the other like a young Child.

Some husbands who feel insecure unknowingly marry someone to parent them. Historically it has been, and still is, more common for women to be viewed as children. When women are considered less important than men, as "unsuccessful acts of procreation," the implication is that they are less than whole. Obviously, this view is not appealing to the many women who want freedom to be whole and act courageously to become that way, often by going to work or back to school.

Mathematically, a marriage in which one person feels incomplete and dependent can be expressed as

$$1\text{ person} + \tfrac{1}{2}\text{ person} \longrightarrow 1\tfrac{1}{2}\text{ persons.}$$

Partners with the *third attitude* feel that marriage is not meant to meld people together (as in the first attitude) but to enhance and enrich each person, so that in the end there are *two unique individuals relating freely and independently*. This often is the formula for companionate marriages. Both partners are free to "do their own thing."

The same attitude may also be expressed when the marriage is for financial convenience. As long as there are no money mix-ups, the two may live together, but as two separate individuals. Modern professional couples often see themselves as free and independent, and they feel comfortable with traveling that takes them away from each other. Their possessions, finances, and bills may be labeled "his" and "hers," instead of "ours." This is often a healthy, friendly marriage, but it may lack passion and ecstacy.

Mathematically, the companionate marriage is expressed as

1 person + 1 person ⟶ 1 person + 1 person.

According to the *fourth attitude,* the relationship between two intimates is sometimes so powerful and dynamic that *the relationship itself can be viewed as a new self.* The partners maintain not only their fullest individuality, but experience a *new personal reality* in the process.

There are really three "selves" in the relationship: you, me, and our relationship. The relationship, with a life of its own, becomes what we call a "third self." Although this can occur in any kind of marriage, most often it is in those where the spiritual or loving views of marriage are strongest.

Mathematically, the relating process might be represented:

1 person + 1 person ⟶ 1 person + 1 person + a third self.

Carl Jung wrote: "The meeting of two personalities is like the contact of two chemical substances; if there is any reaction, both are transformed." A process that begins with two persons meeting, courting, and marrying may eventually generate a third self. This third self (the relationship—the "we-ness") has its own personality and ego states. Couples who have it, know they have it because they know at the deepest levels of being that theirs is a loving, intimate marriage.[3]

Inner core energy and its use

You may be asking yourself how a third self is possible, how you can get the energy to create a loving new marriage or the energy to rebuild an old one. The key is learning how to recognize and use your inner core.

Each of us has a different body and a different personality. All of us also have something in common. We want to live and live in freedom. We want new experiences, we want the chance to analyze situations and make our own decisions. We want to relate to others in meaningful ways. We want close intimacy with a few people and healthy relations with others. Within ourself, which is our body and our personality, is an inner core. This is the part of us that we experience as our deepest self.

The most basic characteristic of the inner core is the *urge to live.* It is this urge, this power source, that energizes us to force our way through the birth canal and to gasp for air. It is this urge that energizes us to fight for our lives when necessary.

In people who are seriously depressed or ill, this urge may be at low ebb. They may express their feelings by saying, "There's nothing to live for" (which translates, "I have no hope"), or "I can't face another day with this pain" (which translates, "I haven't the courage"), or "I'll never get rid of my past" (which translates, "I have no freedom.")

The *urge for freedom* is an essential part of the inner core. The urge to be free releases energies to grow as an individual, to break through archaic ways of thinking, feeling, and acting, and to live and create new environments where freedom from oppression allows for freedom to be oneself and to move into relationships with others that are also free.

The *urge to relate* to other people releases energies to seek them out, to get married, join clubs, have families, develop friends, to play, work, and cooperate. The urge to relate in meaningful ways also releases energies to create "third selves" with other people with whom we can freely be ourselves. Individual freedom and relationship freedom are opposite swings of the same pendulum. The urge and the energies constantly sway us.

The *urge to experience new things* and to analyze the experiences releases energies for exploring both inner and outer worlds, subjectively and objectively. Your ability to experience yourself subjectively through feelings and objectively through analytical thought helps shape you as a person and helps shape your marriage. The new ideas you may have from reading this book have perhaps freed you a bit, brought out your natural courage to change and your hope for the future.

Last, but not least, your *urge to make decisions* is part of your inner core. This urge releases energies to make agreements with yourself and your partner and to carry them out.

These five urges are somewhat like the coals of a fire that generates power. The coals may flare up or die down. But they are always there, in the inner core of the fire.

Energy is power. There are many kinds of physical power—electromagnetic, mechanical, brute strength. There are other, more personal, kinds such as sexual or legal power. There is also the power that comes from money or titles or some other form of prestige. Sometimes a political or religious leader has great power, or power is primarily held by one partner in a marriage. Sometimes the power is in a group, like a group of colleagues or a social or political organization.

But the power in a holistic marriage is a combination of the creative urges of both partners. They have developed their sense of "we" until it has become a "third self." Their energy is released through the power of actions like a tender touch, and through words like, "I've missed you and I'm glad you're home." In a marriage for loving the inner core energies of two people are intermingled to generate new energy. Maybe this hasn't happened yet to you. But it can if you believe the words of Nikos Kazantzakis:

> *By believing passionately in something that still does not exist, we create it. The non-existent is whatever we have not sufficiently desired.*[4]

Three sources of meaning

In releasing the inner core and choosing a "third self," holistic marriage gives profound meaning to life. Faith is what people believe in—their views and values. Hope is what motivates them. Meaning is what they want and need to find. No matter what kind of marriage the future will bring, the search for meaning is a major challenge that every couple will face.

Everyone has the desire to reach out for meaning and feels frustrated or empty if the meaning is not discovered. Everyone also has the freedom to find meaning, and to find it abundantly. I believe this is a responsibility for each person *and* for each couple, and I agree with Martin Buber that "life lived in freedom is personal responsibility or it is a pathetic farce."[5]

Psychiatrist Viktor Frankl believes that the search for meaning is a major life force. He reports that many people are motivated more deeply by a "search for meaning" than by a "search for self."[6] When a situation seems meaningless, people often become bored, or they escalate their feelings until a crisis errupts, or they have a general feeling of dissatisfaction.

Dissatisfaction in marriage is sometimes labeled the "seven year itch" or the "midlife crisis." It is an indication that a couple's original reasons for marrying no longer seem valid to them and the marriage has lost its meaning. Perhaps the views and hopes they originally had were not realistic for long-range goals. Their personal needs were not met; their values did not harmonize.

When people find meaning in their marriages they discover a deep satisfaction. This new-found meaning is often part of a holistic marriage, one of interdependence. Individuals in these marriages find meaning in three ways: in achieving creative tasks, in having positive experiences of love, truth, and beauty, and in learning how to cope with unavoidable suffering.

Many husbands and wives find meaning for themselves as individuals in *creatively achieving a task*—planning it, working on it, completing it. A different meaning is discovered when they creatively achieve a task with a sense of emotional oneness instead of individualism. Planting a vegetable garden *together,* building a house *together,* developing a business *together,* often is a step toward developing a holistic relationship.

So too in positive experiences of love, truth, beauty, or of knowing one or more persons deeply in all their uniqueness, a husband or wife may experience this kind of meaning either as individuals or as a holistic couple. Listening together to the string music of a Beethoven concerto, seeing the sun rise together, or experiencing ecstacy in sexual intercourse are only a few of the many close and positive experiences they can share.

The third area of meaning can be found in *coping with one's own or other people's suffering when it cannot be avoided.* Suffering is often a lonely, isolating experience. Not so for the partners in a holistic marriage. They are not alone and they know it.

When people have freedom from external authorities that stifle and repress, when they have freedom from physical needs that come from poverty or illness, when they have freedom from archaic beliefs that leave an internal residue of fear and inadequacy, then the issue becomes: freedom *from* what *to* what?

The "to what?" can be answered in terms of meaning. Experiences of beauty, achievement, or unavoidable suffering all have meaning when partners discover what the meaning is, or create a meaning. When they do not make the discovery or are not able to create their own meaning, they are in danger of experiencing an existential vacuum—their existence feels empty.

When life seems empty, boring, meaningless, and marriage more like a desert than an oasis, then *commitment* can sustain people until their crisis is past. The commitment can be to a view of marriage, to a life-style, to an intellectual pursuit, to appreciating the past, or to planning the future. More important, the commitment can be to search for or create meanings—what does it mean to be *more* than two individuals married to each other. What does it mean to be *us*? To have a third self that is more than the sum of the two of us?

When the answer begins to emerge, couples often feel new hope, as if a new light were shining on their marriage, a light like daybreak or a full moon or a rainbow after a storm.[7]

People often disagree on whether life in general and marriage in particular has meaning. Some think it has. Because marriage "makes sense" to them, it has purpose and therefore has meaning. Others suffer from a sort of inner emptiness and can find no meaning at all that is worth living for. They say, "My marriage doesn't mean much to me anymore. I don't feel like doing anything about it." People who speak like this often feel powerless. They have given up hoping and have settled for hopelessness.

The power of hope

To hope is to look forward with confidence to a desired result. People live by hope. Hope is as basic to human existence as freedom and courage. When enslaved, we hope for freedom; when filled with fear, we hope for courage.

> *Gloria's husband was on an extended sales trip. One of their three small children had a crippling illness that required almost continuous attention.*

> *I asked her how she managed to cope with the nursing requirements and still feel as if she could keep her head above water. Gloria's response was, "In my mind I see him coming home next week, walking in the door, holding me in his arms, crying with me over Jill, playing again with the twins. I see him doing this, so I have* hope *that I can get through this week. And I can."*

People with hope for the future suffer less in the present. They focus their attention on positive goals and visualize themselves achieving them. Often they do.

Many people stay married because they have hope for the future, not because they are satisfied with the way things are. Many others marry a second or third time because their hope is stronger than their negative experiences. They hope and expect to do better when they remarry, and many of them do. They "learn from experience."

Hope is not a popular word. Some psychologists and philosophers have tended to equate it with "wishful thinking."

One of the earliest case studies of hope is the ancient Greek myth of Pandora, meaning "all gifted." It tells how Pandora, as the first woman, was made in heaven with every god contributing something that would make her perfect. Venus gave her beauty, Mercury gave her persuasion, and so forth. In one version of the myth, Zeus, king of the gods, sends the insatiably curious Pandora to earth as a curse (in another version, Pandora is sent as a blessing). Pandora opens a jar out of curiosity and all the evils of the world escape to plague humanity; only hope remains.[8]

A common sexual stereotype is that hoping is what women are supposed to do, and courage is expected of men. What a fallacy! In marriage, one or both partners may be hopeful. If only one is, then he or she will work toward bringing more happiness into the situation even though the other is trying to undermine it. If both are hopeful, they are likely to experience a strong sense of power.

If both feel hopeless, they feel powerless, inadequate, and depressed together. They feel like giving up, as if there is "no way to turn." They recover hope when they are able to renew their energies. Forty-year-old Leon discovered hope for his marriage after nearly ruining it:

> *For years I've been playing around, first with one woman, then another. I get really excited when choosing someone almost as young as my daughters. Naturally, I'm not available if they want to marry me because I won't divorce my wife. She wouldn't let me.*

So these young chicks start chasing me. Threatening suicide and all that jazz. Maybe it's my money they want or the excitement I give them. Maybe it's because I know how to make a woman happy, maybe they're just looking for another father. Maybe I'm just looking for a daughter who will love me, my own don't and my wife's a mess.

But I'm fed up with chasing and being chased. I'm fed up with myself. I want to get my life together before it's too late. Once upon a time we had an okay marriage. I want to get some romance back into it. I want to learn how to be friends with my wife instead of being such a tramp.

Marriage is very much like a pilgrimage, a search for a convenient and comfortable life, a life of shared values, romance, or companionship. Some couples search for transcendent moments of love, for peak experiences that give meaning to their marriage and to all of life. In a loving marriage the pilgrimage leads to all this and more: the creation of a third self.

To achieve this kind of marriage some freedom from the past is usually necessary. It is also necessary to face the present with courage and look to the future with hope. When people do this, they often succeed in creating a marriage that is a truly loving relationship. They contribute to the ongoing and positive evolution of marriage.

Chapter 10

"What do you like about our marriage?"

"Well, what I like best is that we're not the same as we used to be."

"Probably it's because we don't just stand still or mark time."

"That's right. After all these years we still seem to be moving ahead."

"I wonder what it will be like in five years."

"Me, too. Shall we decide or just wait and see what happens?"

"Let's not wait. Let's plan ahead."

"How would you like it to be?"

"There's only one thing I know for sure. That's for our loving to keep on growing."

"Come here, honey. I'm falling in love with you all over again!"

You and Your Marriage: The Future

Perhaps we have all felt that it would be great to fall in love again. Some people believe this means falling in love with a person to whom they are not married. But in a loving marriage it is possible to fall in love over and over again with the same person. The excitements may sometimes fade, yet they build up again when two people anticipate the future, as well as when they enjoy the present and solve its problems.

Loving couples need to plan for the future, just as they need to understand their past and focus on the here-and-now present of their marriages. Planning for the future takes energy, it takes the capacity to visualize the best that can be, and it takes a willingness to set goals and work toward them. The exercises in this chapter are designed to help you do just that. The Transactional Analysis section will include theory and application for making contracts, creating a "third self," and discovering inner core energies.

Out of focus

Falling in love again does not happen if couples focus on the negatives of the past or present or refuse to look to the future with hope.

I remember a cartoon of two old persons obviously sick and in pain. One was saying to the other, "If I had known I was going to live so long, I would have taken better care of myself." That's an issue for each person to face, each couple to explore.

When people choose to be past oriented, they frequently focus on what was said or done last year, or the year before, or in the dim past. Their thinking is out of focus for present and future living.

> *Julia, an attractive, competent, 50-year-old widow, often said she would like to meet someone whom she might eventually feel like marrying. However, each man she met was compared unfavorably with her husband. "No one could ever be the same, with the same hands and same face." Because no man could ever be the same, each one was automatically rejected before Julia had time to find out whether she wanted to be seriously involved or not.*
>
> *Alan also focused on the past. "When we got divorced, my wife took every cent I had. You can bet your sweet life I'll never get involved again. Furthermore, if I think about it long enough and hard enough, I'll get even with her."*

Other couples live primarily in the now. They act as if they had neither past or future. The pleasure of the moment is their concern. They don't want to look ahead or think about the rational consequences of their current behavior. Sue and George often argue about how to spend their money. "I want a boat," he argues. "I want an Oriental rug," she responds. "OK," they agree, "let's buy both and figure out later how to pay for them."

Still other couples build up anxieties by focusing on possible future catastrophes. "Suppose the children get into drugs," or "What if your mother comes to live with us?" or "What if you lose your job, or I get sick?" In frustration or despair, such couples may give up trying. They may feel hopeless and refuse to think about the future at all.

Other people explore only the immediate future—the vacation they'll take next week, the house they'll buy next year, the travel they'll do after retirement, and so on. This kind of planning has value, but it may not take into consideration the wider context in which they live.

Planning the future in a meaningful, loving context requires the free flow of a couple's energies. They need to learn how to channel their energies so they can cope with the past, live in the present, and look forward to the future with enthusiasm and hope.

Energy flows and energy blocks

To hope and plan for the future all couples need energy. Yet often, in the wake of day-to-day problems and frustrations, they lose the energy they need. This loss generally occurs in one of three ways.

Energy and action are *blocked* by some external force, like a society that does not allow equal opportunities for everyone or laws that restrict what certain people can do. Other external forces that restrict couples are problems such as immigration quotas that keep couples apart, or financial requirements that restrict them from buying a house.

Energy is *drained* by physically exhausting jobs or continuing emotional demands. A handicapped child or an elderly parent needing constant care drain energy. So do situations such as commuting in heavy traffic, living in a humid climate, being faced with unsolvable problems, or having poor health.

Energy is *restricted* by internal fear, guilt, and anxiety. When people have negative feelings, such as low self-esteem, they tend to tighten up. They restrict themselves from developing their potential and hold back on making decisions. This increases that anxiety.

Visualize a river flowing downstream. The energy of the flow can be *blocked* by a dam, *drained* off by a lot of irrigation ditches, or *restricted* if the banks cave in and the flow is reduced because of narrowness. The Latin word for anxiety, *angustia,* literally means "narrowness."

So, too, in marriage. The views we hold, the life-styles we live or try to live, may block our energy, drain it off, or restrict it. In marriages where the partners think of themselves as a *couple* in the process of growing, rather than as two individuals who happen to be married, energy flows freely.

When blocks occur the partners remove the blocks by open discussion of the issues and by sharing their feelings, accepting what can't be changed and changing what can. When their energy is drained, they renew it by resting or playing. Sometimes they ignore the doorbell or phone just to be quiet together. Sometimes they go to bed early, or sleep late, or find some other way for their energy to be renewed.

When either feels anxious or when both do, as, for example, when a child is ill or injured, or a job is lost, or an operation is anticipated, they help relieve inner restrictions when they share their fears with each other. They trust that their fears will be accepted, not denied or ridiculed.

It is in moments like this, when an atmosphere of acceptance prevails, that marriage seems most worthwhile. Energy to enjoy or energy to solve other problems flows again. New meaning and fresh hope is experienced. It's like crawling out of a cold, dark tunnel. In the words of Dag Hammarskjold:

> *You wake from dreams of doom and—for a moment—you* know:
> *beyond all the noise and the gestures, the only real thing, love's calm unwavering flame in the half-light of an early dawn.*

Knowing this is possible day after day enables partners to make new decisions.

Deciding to enjoy

It is clear that the future of any marriage is largely influenced by past events, by family and social tradition, and also by decisions made in the present.

Making decisions for the future is simple for some couples. They are not afraid to make mistakes and learn from them. They may try to do what they consider right, but they are not compulsive about trying to be perfect couples. Couples who do expect perfection in their marriage often delay decisions indefinitely and thus lose much of their self-activating power. Other couples find it hard to make decisions when marriage problems continue month after month and don't get better. The longer the problem persists, the more insecure they feel about the future.

One wife, who had been in a marriage counseling group and who had become autonomous in the process, described decision making in the following way:

> *What I decide* now *will affect my marriage tomorrow. If I decide to hold on to an old resentment or an unreal fantasy, my decision will interfere with future joy. If I decide to let go of old resentments and unreal fantasies, my decisions will enhance the possibilities for future joys.*

Not all of life produces joy, yet decision making can be a positive experience. Four attitudes are possible in any decision-making process. Two of them offer possibilities of joy; two offer only misery. The attitudes are

1. Do it and enjoy it.
2. Do it and don't enjoy it.
3. Don't do it and enjoy it.
4. Don't do it and don't enjoy it.[2]

The *process* of decision making can be rewarding even if the decision itself, such as what to do with a senile parent, a handicapped child, or a destructive marriage, is painful.

The enjoy attitudes can be applied to almost any issue. For example, a sexual affirmation plan may be built on the idea of sometimes "doing it and enjoying it" and sometimes "not doing it and enjoying the not doing." In the latter case, to enjoy the "not doing" is not to get even with a partner or make the partner feel bad in some way. It is to postpone pleasure until the timing is better or the energy level is higher.

The not-enjoying attitudes are poor alternatives. Submitting to the inevitable and "not enjoying it" is no fun. So, too, is refusal and then feeling guilty, angry, or sad over "not doing it."

These attitudes can be adopted in any problem situation. When couples have problems with money, they can bring any of these same four attitudes to their budgeting process or spending habits. So, too, with vacation time, work time, and on and on.

It takes awareness and sometimes courage and hope to decide to enjoy certain situations. It also takes awareness and sometimes courage and hope to get out of other situations and enjoy the getting out. It can be done. People can decide and act in the present so that the future will be more loving than the past.

Visualizing the good

The capacity for imagining the future is one of the more interesting assets people have. Seemingly this is a uniquely human characteristic. Couples can envision what they have not seen, and their visions can be positive or negative. There is no doubt that people often make themselves ill by using their imagination to create visions of catastrophe. They also make themselves well by visualizing the opposite.

At the time of this writing, one of the most dramatic ways of creating good health has been demonstrated by Carl Simonton, M.D., and his wife Stephanie at the Oncology Clinic in Fort Worth, Texas. They have developed a technique that is sometimes effective in curing cancer if the patient cooperates in specific ways. Simonton's techniques include standard medical treatment, giving the patient information, and providing psychotherapy so that the patient becomes aware that *the illness meets some emotional need.* This part of the treatment includes relaxation and visualizing techniques in which strong white cells are pictured destroying the cancer cells.

If this seems farfetched to you, then experiment with this simple exercise of mind over body.

> *Close your eyes and* imagine *that in your hands you have a ripe juicy orange. Hold it, smell it, start to peel it. Slowly peel back the skin and feel the juice running out on your hand. Now break it apart and put a segment in your mouth. Taste the juice as it runs down your throat. Now take another segment as you taste how sweet and juicy it is.*
>
> *Keep your eyes closed and imagine you have a lemon. Cut it in two with a knife. Pick up one half, put it in your mouth and suck it.*[3]

If you're like most people, you probably felt your mouth pucker up because of what you *imagined* you saw and tasted. Real-life situations are more complex than lemons. In real life you may not have all the facts you need for an accurate projection of the future. Nevertheless, even without all the facts, you are still strongly affected by the way you imagine the future is going to be.

If partners view their future differently, perhaps because they have different views of how their marriage has been in the past, then they need to acknowledge the conflict and try to work it out in a positive way.

A version of the Simontons' technique can be applied to this kind of unhealthy marriage. For it to be effective, each partner must first own up to his or her responsibility for the things that went wrong. This owning up requires more than an intellectual "Yes, I am responsible for myself and my part in this marriage." It requires an emotional acceptance at the core of being.

Next comes positive visualization—not of healthy cells fighting unhealthy ones, but of partners fusing together, then separating, then fusing again, and again. As a unit, the two need to be *seen in process,* joining together, working together, loving together. The two also need to be visualized as individuals, leaving each other, working and playing separately, becoming autonomous, then coming together again.

Future Rating and Our Views of Marriage

Use this rating process to focus on the *future* of your marriage, not on the present or the past. What direction does it seem to be taking?

As a convenient relationship it seems to be going

As a spiritual relationship it seems to be going

As a romantic relationship it seems to be going

As a companionate relationship it seems to be going

As a loving relationship it seems to be going

Do you like the way your marriage seems to be going? If not, what would each of you need to do so that the future would be more joyful?

Our Marriage Will Be For . . .

Imagine you are in a debate about the future of your marriage. Select the view of marriage that you prefer. Then make an opening statement, outline the points you wish to make, and close with a summarizing argument.

Opening statement: I hope the future of our marriage will be . . .

Points to be made: I want this because . . .

1.

2.

3.

4.

5.

Closing argument: "In summary . . ."

Now study what you have written. Are you clear about what you think? Would your arguments convince someone else who has a different view?

Marriage Styles Now and Then

Change may take many years or happen rather rapidly. Consider how the six marriage styles—in the past, present, and future—were or might be part of your marriage:

Our marriage styles	*In the past*	*Now*	*Future options*
Traditional			
Directed by personal interest			

Influenced by institutions

Nondirected

Group or communal

Holistic (third self)

How Much Change Can You Take?

Dr. Thomas H. Holmes, professor of psychiatry at the University of Washington, has devised a scale assigning point value to changes, both good and bad, that often affect us.[4] When enough changes occur during one year to add up to 300, a danger point has been reached. In the population he studied, 80 percent of the people who exceeded 300 became seriously depressed, had heart attacks, or suffered other serious illnesses.

Life change	*Points*
Death of spouse	100
Divorce	73
Marital separation	65
Jail term	63
Death of family member	63
Personal injury or illness	53
Marriage	50
Fired from job	47
Marital reconciliation	45
Retirement	45
Change in health of family member	44
Pregnancy	40
Sex difficulties	39
Gain of new family member	39
Change in financial status	38
Death of close friend	37
Change to different kind of work	36

Change in number of arguments with spouse	35
Foreclosure of mortgage or loan	30
Change in work responsibilities	29
Son or daughter leaving home	29
Trouble with in-laws	29
Outstanding personal achievement	28
Wife beginning or stopping work	26
Beginning or ending school	26
Revision of personal habits	24
Trouble with boss	23
Change in residence	20
Change in schools	20
Vacation	13
Minor violations of law	11

When you evaluate the stresses in your life, what does it show and what do you need to do?

Life Line of the Future

Now ____ At death

Along the line above write in some of the things you hope to do this month, this year, within five years, ten years, twenty years, and so forth.

Next, under each of those goals, jot down how your life-style could change as a result of working toward the goals or achieving them.

Star the goals that are particularly important to you. Fix them in your mind. Visualize yourself achieving them. Repeat this visualization daily.

Mathematics of Your Marriage

Formulas in relationships	*Situations when I felt or acted this way*	*Situations when my partner felt or acted this way*
Formula 1: $\frac{1}{2} + \frac{1}{2} \longrightarrow 1$	________	________
	________	________
	________	________
Formula 2: $\frac{1}{2} + 1 \longrightarrow 1\frac{1}{2}$	________	________
	________	________
	________	________
Formula 3: $1 + 1 \longrightarrow 1 + 1$	________	________
	________	________
	________	________
Formula 4: $1 + 1 \longrightarrow 1 + 1 + 1$	________	________
	________	________
	________	________

Future planning: As you study the patterns above, begin your plan for improving the future. Although many couples will occasionally interact on the basis of the first two formulas, the healthiest marriages are those characterized primarily by the third formula, an independent relationship, or the fourth formula, an interdependent relationship of choice where a third self can develop because of love and respect.

The freedom turntable

The word *tracking* is sometimes used to refer to the way people focus on a certain form of relationship. It also refers to tracks that trains or trolley cars run on. This section combines the two ideas.

Consider four possible tracks: large organizations, small family groups, couples, and individuals. Some people devote energy to all these tracks. Some stay on one or two tracks and ignore the others.

We all belong to several larger communities: humanity at large, the national political and social scene, our geographical region, our town or city, and so forth. In contrast, most of us are also very concerned with individual growth and continue to be so; this trend has been developing and expanding ever since the Renaissance.

Two other tracks we can take are to a family group or to a couple. A couple is a twosome such as married partners or two close friends. Any twosome, like any other "relationship" track, can be healing or hurting, growing or static, exciting or boring, hating or loving. Only if a couple is a deeply loving relationship can a third self develop. The third self transcends routine relationships and the gain and pain of the marketplace. A third self provides meaning at the inner core.

These four relationship tracks are like trolley car tracks that run into a turntable, as the trolley cars do in San Francisco. Some people get stuck on one track and go around and around. Seldom do they experience the new growth that comes from going on to other tracks.

Edward, for example, was a "joiner." He was very active in social and political organizations as well as in his corporation. His wife, Elizabeth, preferred to spend her time in pursuits that led to self-growth. Both complained that they didn't have enough time for their friends or family or even for each other. The problem was that he was stuck on the organizational track, she on the track of individualism. Intellectually they knew the other dimensions existed, but they did not perceive that they were free to experience them.

The Freedom Turntable

For this exercise, imagine a turntable called "freedom," with the different tracks running into it.

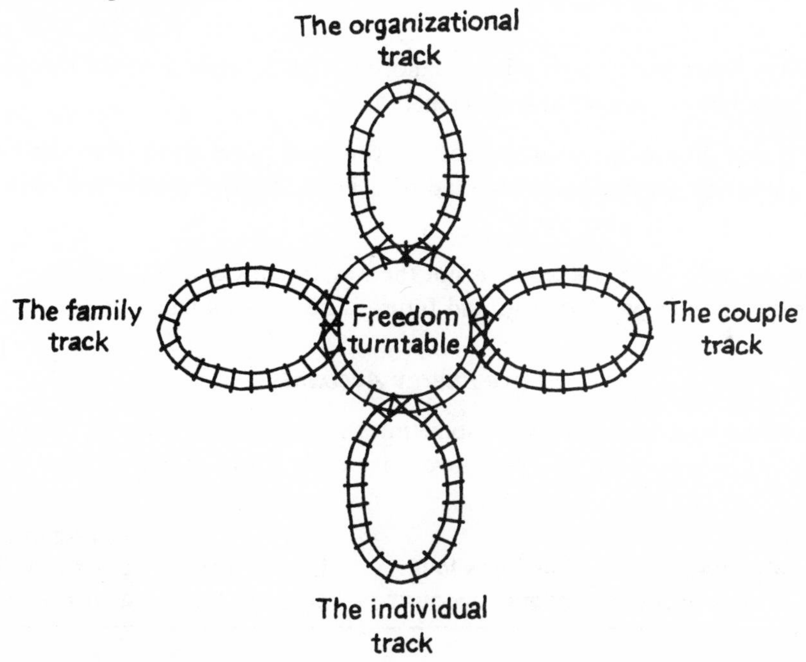

Consider how much interest and energy you put into each track. Rate yourself and partner from 1 (low) to 10 (high).

My energy involvement

on the organizational track

on the individualism track

on the family track

on the couple track

My partner's energy involvement

on the organizational track

on the individualism track

on the family track

on the couple track

Are either you or your partner ignoring a track? How are your energy expenditures similar and different?

If you do not like what you see, do you need to get on the freedom turntable and get free from one kind of overinvolvement so that you can move onto another track?

All tracks have value. Either/or is not the way to go. Continual assessment of the tracks in your past, present, and future is needed in a marriage for loving.

Love Energy Accounts

In any marriage, resentments are sometimes stored up until pressure develops and conflict erupts. So, too, with love. Like other forms of energy, love can

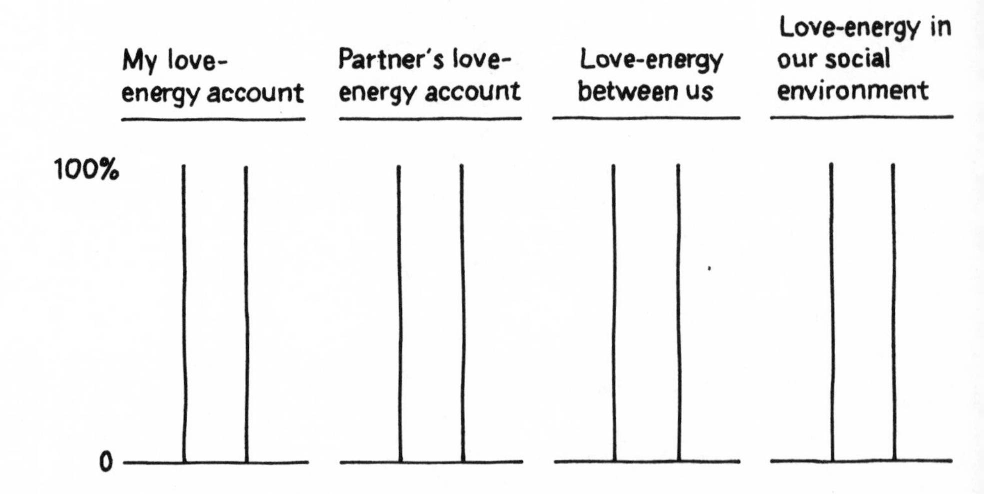

be accumulated and stored—inside an individual, inside a marriage or family, even inside a culture.

Imagine you have a love energy account, somewhat like a bank account, or a thermometer with an upper limit of 100°.

If any of your love energy accounts are low, what plans do you need to make *now* to increase your love in the future?

You and Your Energy Losses

Review the energy patterns in your own marriage. Note especially those situations that drain, block, or constrict your energy.

Situation	*Drains energy*	*Blocks energy*	*Constricts energy*
______________	( )	( )	( )
______________	( )	( )	( )
______________	( )	( )	( )
______________	( )	( )	( )
______________	( )	( )	( )

Now list situations your partner or potential partner might view as leading to an energy loss.

Situation	*Drains energy*	*Blocks energy*	*Constricts energy*
______________	( )	( )	( )
______________	( )	( )	( )
______________	( )	( )	( )
______________	( )	( )	( )
______________	( )	( )	( )

If possible, discuss this exercise with your partner after you have done it. Find out how well you know the person you're married to.

Meanings in Your Marriage

Analyze how you, *as a couple,* have found meaning in the past, how you are currently finding it, and how you could find it in the future.

Meaning in beauty:

past experiences

at present

future possibilities

Meaning in achievements:

past experiences

at present

future possibilities

Meaning in unavoidable suffering:

past experiences

at present

future possibilities

Review the above and consider what your *past* experiences have freed you to do and be. What *current* situations call for you to be courageous? What *future* possibilities do you have that will be helped by hope?

Setting goals for marriage investments

To set a goal is to look toward the future. The first step is to catch a glimpse of something that is possible. The next is to make plans that will lead toward reaching the goal. Then comes action on the basis of the plans and often the readjustment of plans during the process. When the goal is achieved, there is a sense of satisfaction. The goal has been reached. Then other goals may take priority. Or you may decide on a period of rest, like a willow tree resting during the winter.

In any marriage, partners have both individual and joint goals. Sometimes these are in harmony, sometimes not. Sometimes they seem like small goals; other times they are tremendous. Occasionally, they are distorted and out of proportion.

A common distortion is the power struggle over which TV show to watch. One partner may have the goal of watching a sports event; the other partner's goal may be to watch a ballet. If they don't work out an acceptable compromise, resentments are likely to develop.

The capacity to look ahead to goals that both agree to and to foresee conflicting goals is part of the challenge of any marriage.

Setting goals and achieving goals are quite different. One difference is the amount of energy that is involved. Achieving goals often requires a major investment. For example, the investment may involve financial energy, as when deciding to move, return to school, or take a vacation. Or the investment may involve time, as when deciding to talk things out instead of delaying or avoiding "until there is more time."

Many couples fight over what kinds of investments they will make—in themselves, in each other, and in their marriage. Often they are stuck on a particular track. Jeanette, a forty-year-old college educated wife, complained:

> *We've spent years accumulating* things, *providing more and more* things *for our children. We've always put them first. If we go on this way in the future, our marriage relationship won't have any depth. We'll be part of a family but with no ties between the two of us. The problem is, if we start to focus on us, it's going to* cost *us something. Time away from the kids, away from the job, away from the bridge club, and so on. It might even cost us our self-esteem. We've prided ourselves on being a good mom and dad. What if it turns out that we're a terrible husband and wife! It would hurt to find that out. Also, if we focus on just the two of us, some of our friends and family might not like it. That would be another cost, an expensive one!*

Investments are always much higher when people risk changing their views about marriage and their life-styles. However, the return on the investment is also likely to be greater. When people choose to take this risk, they need courage and hope to see them through. They need the skills for making contracts.

Contracts for change

There are three areas in which marriage partners may decide to establish contracts.

They can use contracts to *change behavior.* For example, they can agree to stop procrastinating and to start completing projects on time.

They can also establish contracts to change *feelings.* For example, one partner can agree to stop feeling like a victim when criticized, and to start evaluating criticism realistically.

Couples can even establish contracts to decrease *psychosomatic symptoms,* such as overweight or high blood pressure, and to have more respect for their bodies and their feelings.

Many people refuse to make valid contracts because of a feeling of "I can't." These people almost never reach their goals because they are tied to destructive or going-nowhere scripts. One purpose of learning how to make contracts is to increase personal OKness and the OKness of others, especially that of your partner.[5]

Another purpose is to increase the loving between you. The words "I love you," are different from, "I am loving you." The latter phrase is active and implies *doing* something, not just *feeling* something. Feelings are fine and to feel loving is certainly better than not feeling loving. But there can be more than just feeling. Positive feelings motivate couples to action; negative feelings may do the same.

> *"I feel so lonesome for you when you're out of town," sighed Sarah. "Maybe so," responded Louis, "but I wish you'd stop feeling so much and get to* doing *something like picking up the broom and cleaning up the place instead of reading all the time. You said you didn't want to work, that you wanted to stay home and keep house. Well, do it then! I know it isn't exciting and if you'd rather work and get someone to clean, OK. But stop just sitting there and feeling bad.* Do something!"

Couples who want to change their marriages have to do more than wish and want. They have to risk. Risk takes courage, and it takes hope that success is possible. When people are acting courageously, they are often afraid. Yet underneath the fear is hope—hope that things can and will improve. And they will improve as goals are set and contracts are made.

Contracts are basic to Transactional Analysis. They set the guidelines for what is wanted and the details—much like a legal contract—explaining why, when, where, how, and so forth. Contracts need to be clear, precise, and direct. They also need to be based on realistic goals that can be reached by realistic means.

For instance, a couple may make a realistic contract about looking more attractive, but they are not being realistic if they expect, at age fifty, to turn back the clock and look like persons of twenty. Realistic contracts can be made about feeling better, but it is not realistic for people to expect to feel better without changing their life-style, job, or the way they structure their time.

To achieve a goal, some kind of external or internal change is necessary. The willingness to change is thus a major requirement. Many partners are for change—but each wants the other partner to do all the changing. Yet in every contract, some kind of personal change is necessary.

A couple that is trying to improve their communication, for example, must stop blaming each other for "not understanding." Each needs to take responsibility for his or her own side of the transaction. Each should experiment with being straightforward and direct rather than continue being indirect and playing games.

"What could *I* do differently to achieve our goals?" is a continuing question for loving partners.

What Do You Want to Enhance Your Marriage?

Hope and courage are not enough. Action is needed. For any positive change, couples need first to wish, then to want, then to decide how to get what they want.

List five things you want and five that your partner wants that would enhance your marriage.

I Want	*My priority*	*Partner wants*	*Partner's priority*
1. ____________	( )	1. ____________	( )
2. ____________	( )	2. ____________	( )
3. ____________	( )	3. ____________	( )

4. ____________	( )	4. ____________	( )
5. ____________	( )	5. ____________	( )

Assign priorities by putting a number in the parentheses to show what you each want most and least.

Now, list each one again, and after each indicate what it might cost (in time, energy, money, and so forth) and what you might gain.

My wants	*Possible cost*	*Possible gains*
1. ____________	____________	____________
2. ____________	____________	____________
3. ____________	____________	____________
4. ____________	____________	____________
5. ____________	____________	____________

Partner's wants	*Possible cost*	*Possible gains*
1. ____________	____________	____________
2. ____________	____________	____________
3. ____________	____________	____________
4. ____________	____________	____________
5. ____________	____________	____________

As you look over the possible costs and gains, do your wants change? Do your priorities change?

How do you feel when you compare your lists? How will you assign priorities if they are in conflict?

What Do You Need to Do?

Close your eyes and relax. Then let words come into your awareness that describe what you would need to do to get what you want in your marriage. You may want to use the most important "wants" that you identified in the previous exercise.

What I want for my marriage in the future is

What I need to do to get what I want is

Evaluate this list of actions you could take and star the ones that are practical and possible.

What Are You Willing to Do?

Many couples know what they need to do to enhance a marriage, but they are not willing to do it. One partner may be aware of habitually talking too much yet not be willing to stop "always trying to get in the last word." Or one partner may be aware of withdrawing a lot—not sharing ideas and feelings with the other, and not being willing to risk new patterns. How about you?

Record your list, or make up a new one, and evaluate—not what you want to do, or need to do, but what you're really willing to do.

What I want in my marriage is

What I'm willing to do to get what I want is

Think it over. Are you being realistic? If not, change what you want. You won't get it until you're willing to work at it.

How Will Your Success Show?

When people make contracts and achieve them, their success is likely to show in some way—their eyes might sparkle, they might laugh more often, they might look more attractive.

Sometimes, when one partner changes, the other one does not notice. It may take energy and courage to say, "Hey, look at me! I'm different."

Think of one of the things you want. How would your success show if you got it? What positive thing could you do if no one notices?

One of my wants is

My success would show by

What I could do if no one notices is

To draw attention to positive changes is not conceit. It is a way to have your changes reinforced by others.

How Might You Avoid Getting What You Want?

Many people do not achieve their goals because they undermine or sabotage themselves in some way. They may want to affirm their sexuality and sabotage themselves by getting too tired. They may want to save money for a vacation and sabotage themselves by buying things they don't need just because they're on sale.

List some wants and potential sabotages:

One of my wants is	*I might sabotage myself by*	*Others might sabotage me by*
______	______	______
______	______	______
______	______	______
______	______	______
______	______	______

In the case of sabotage, you need an alternative plan of action. What could yours be?

What Strengths Do You Have for Keeping Contracts?

Many people are not aware of all the skills, talents, abilities, and natural gifts they have that could help them fulfill their contracts.

What are your strengths, those you have and those you could develop?

My present strengths include	*I could use them more effectively by*
______________________	______________________
______________________	______________________
______________________	______________________
______________________	______________________

My potential strengths include	*I could develop them by*
______________________	______________________
______________________	______________________
______________________	______________________
______________________	______________________

How are your feelings of power and hope as you review your strengths?

Falling in Love Again

Is it possible to fall in love again and again with the same person—your partner? Do you want to?

Many people are thrilled by the possibility of falling in love and being loved in return. If you are one of them and want to contract for falling in love again, try answering the following questions.

What would I be willing to do?

How would I measure my success?

How might I sabotage myself?

What strengths could I use to succeed?

Creating a Third Self

Transactions between partners are usually diagramed as in the chapter, "You and Your Marriage: The Present." When a third self develops, the diagram is different. The third self has its own personality and its "ego states." It consists of a combination of what each partner *gives* to the relationship. Each person also *takes* from it. Like money in a savings account, the more you put in, the higher the earnings.

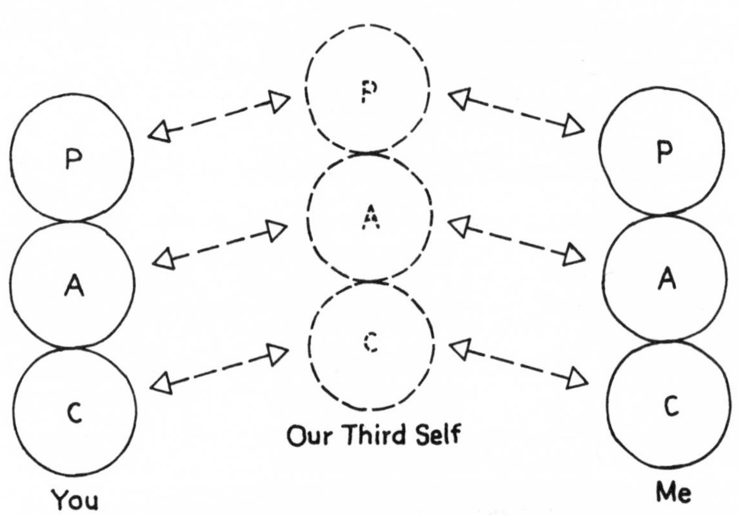

The third-self relationship of intimacy
(Note that the arrows point both ways)

Mutual acceptance creates the climate in which a third self can grow. Acceptance often leads to unconditional love and nonstop giving and receiving. For many people an awareness of God in the relationship accelerates the process. Consider what you could do.

What I give or could give to our marriage to create a third self: ___________

____

____

What my partner gives or could give to our marriage to create a third self: __

____

____

What I could receive from a third self that would strengthen me as a person:

____

____

____

What my partner could receive from a third self that would be strengthening:

____

____

____

Discovering Inner Core Energies

In an individual, inner core energies can be blocked from any or all ego states or can be open to any or all. When blocked,[6] a person does not have the normal sense of power that comes with experiencing and using the inner core urges: to live, to be free, to relate to others in meaningful ways, to have new experiences and be able to understand them, and to make decisions and commitments.

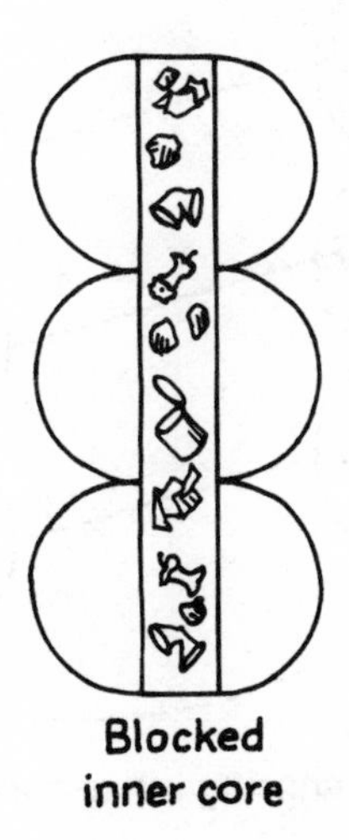

Blocked inner core

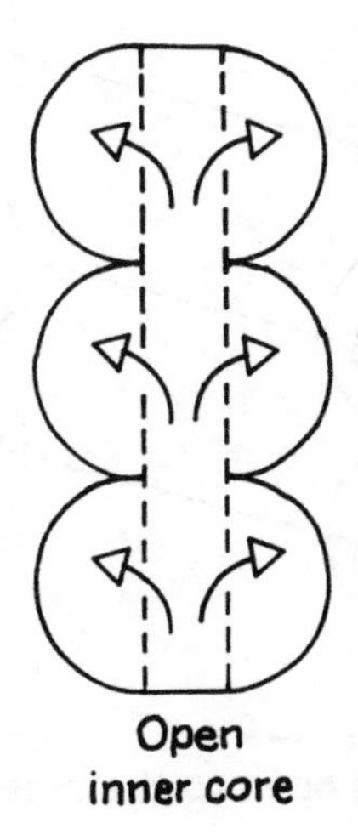

Open inner core

When people are open to their inner cores, they experience these urges intensely; they have a passionate desire to live fully.

My urges	*Intensity of each urge*			*What I need to do to be open to my inner core*
	Weak	*Moderate*	*Strong*	
To live	( )	( )	( )	________
To be free	( )	( )	( )	________
To relate to others	( )	( )	( )	________
To have new experiences	( )	( )	( )	________
To make and keep commitments	( )	( )	( )	________

Ask your partner to do the same exercise, then share your discoveries.

Sharing Inner Core Energies

The awareness of inner core urges and the energy they create in "myself, yourself, and ourself" is an exciting new awareness for a loving marriage. Shared

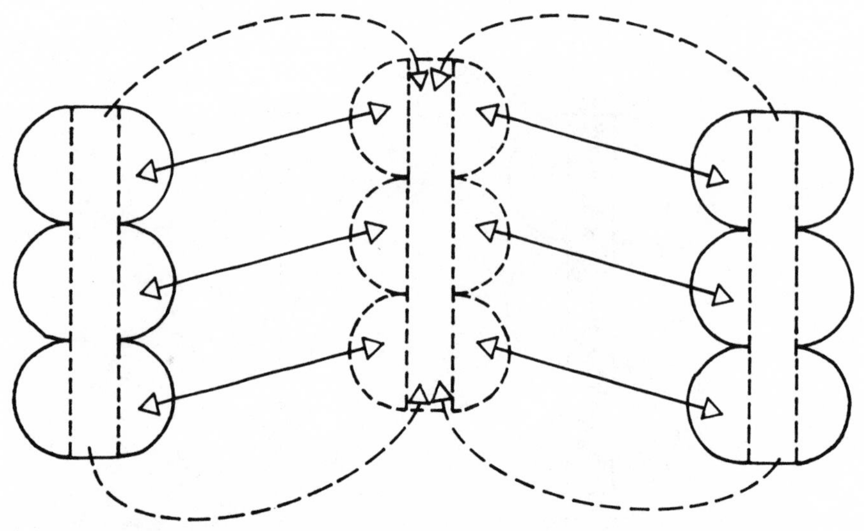

Ego states open to the inner core and sharing inner-core energies

values and meanings become more important than individual desires and needs. A sense of "we-ness," in which "I" am fully "I" and "you" are fully "you," is experienced in power and glory. Inner core energies are exchanged.

Our third self personality traits	*What we each give of ourselves to create our third self*	*Third self inner core energies that we experience*	*What we each give of our inner cores to our third self*
______	______	______	______
______	______	______	______
______	______	______	______
______	______	______	______
______	______	______	______

Now rejoice in what you already have and in what you can release. Your marriage is for loving. Go ahead and love.

Epilogue: Super Living

Some people have hope, have zest—not just for surviving but for "super-living." This is possible because they are conscious of the future toward which they are drawn. They see the future not as an escape *from* the present, but as freedom leading *to* a new kind of fulfillment.

This kind of future fulfillment *may* be that of holistic, loving marriages. These will be couples who work through their unhealthy dependencies on each other and who give up their angry rebellious independencies from each other. They will experience a fundamental sense of peace and joy. They feel centered. They will be a part of what Teilhard de Chardin calls "human convergence."[1]

This kind of marriage will be a form of *co-evolution.* To move this way will require awareness of the universality of freedom. It will require motivation and courage. It will require hope and a deep-rooted, passionate zest to get on with life.

We will change. No doubt about it. We have the choice. We can choose to be passive, simply accepting what comes in the future, or we can choose to be active, directing and designing the future together. Hope springs and gives a glimpse of eternity. Now is the time to celebrate the future.

NOTES

Part One

1. Copyright © 1922, 1950 by Edna St. Vincent Millay, from *Collected Poems* (New York: Harper & Row), p. 128.

Chapter 1

1. As I am more familiar with the Western world than I am with the Eastern world, many of my examples reflect only the Western hemisphere.

Chapter 2

1. From Leonard Cottrell, *Life under the Pharaohs* (New York: Holt, Rinehart & Winston, 1960), p. 77.
2. Quoted in Simone de Beauvoir, *The Second Sex,* trans. H. M. Parshley (New York: Knopf, 1953), p. 74.
3. Palladas, *Historia Lausiaca.*
4. Dionysius of Halicarnassus, in *The Roman Antiquities,* trans. E. Cary (Cambridge, Mass.: Harvard U. Press, 1937), vol. 1, pp. 381 ff.
5. Valerius Maximus, quoted in Julia O'Faolain and Laura Martines, eds., *Not in God's Image* (New York: Harper & Row, 1973), p. 37.
6. Caesar Augustus, quoted in O'Faolain and Martines, eds., *Not in God's Image,* p. 47.
7. Tertullian PL 1, 1418b–19a *De cultu feminarum,* libri duo I, 1.
8. Quoted from *Le Menagier de Paris* in O'Faolain and Martines, eds., *Not in God's Image,* p. 168.
9. H. G. Wells, *The Outline of History* (New York: Garden City Books, 1949), vol. 2, pp. 752–753.
10. Georgia Harkness, *John Calvin, the Man and His Ethic* (New York: Holt, 1931), p. 151.
11. Abigail Adams, quoted in Eleanor Flexner, *Century of Struggle* (Cambridge, Mass.: Belknap Press, 1968), p. 15.
12. Erich Fromm, *Fear of Freedom* (London: Routledge & Kegan Paul Ltd., 1942), pp. 19–88.

Chapter 3

1. Named after J. P. Morgan, the American financier.
2. The current rate for a West German bride is $1,500; for a bridegroom it is $1,250. To get work permits and permanent residences, they arrange to marry citizens of West Germany. Lloyd Shearer, "Intelligence Report," *Oakland Tribune,* 11 December 1977.

3. Abraham H. Maslow, *Religions, Values, and Peak Experiences* (New York: Viking, 1970), p. 59.
4. Jose Ortega y Gassett, *On Love* (Cleveland: World, 1961), p. 51.
5. Ruth Stein, "When First We Met," *San Francisco Chronicle,* 14 February 1977.
6. Muriel James and Louis Savary, *The Heart of Friendship* (New York: Harper & Row, 1976), p. 61.
7. Julian Hawthorne, *Nathaniel Hawthorne and His Wife: A Biography* (1884; reprint ed., Hamden, Conn.: The Shoestring Press, 1968), p. 71.

Chapter 4

1. Harvey Cox, *The Feast of Fools* (Cambridge, Mass.: Harvard U. Press, 1969), pp. 15, 240.
2. Eric Berne, *Transactional Analysis in Psychotherapy* (New York: Grove Press, 1961), pp. 17–43.
3. Muriel James, *The OK Boss* (Reading, Mass.: Addison-Wesley, 1975), pp. 130 ff.
4. See Muriel James and Dorothy Jongeward, *Born to Win: Transactional Analysis with Gestalt Experiments* (Reading, Mass.: Addison-Wesley, 1971), pp. 70–75.

Part Two

1. From "Honey and Salt" in *Honey and Salt,* copyright © 1963 by Carl Sandburg. (New York: Harcourt Brace Jovanovich), p. 3.

Chapter 5

1. Eric Hoffer, *The Passionate State of Mind* (New York: Harper & Row, 1955), p. 73.
2. *Luther's Commentary on Genesis,* trans. J. Theodore Mueller (Grand Rapids, Mich.: Zondervan, 1958), p. 18.
3. Muriel James and Dorothy Jongeward, *Born to Win: Transactional Analysis with Gestalt Experiments* (Reading, Mass.: Addison-Wesley, 1971), p. 274. See also Hugh Prather, *Notes on Love and Courage* (Garden City, New York: Doubleday, 1977), and Rollo May, *The Courage to Create* (New York: Norton, 1975), pp. 12–21.
4. Erik Erikson, *Insight and Responsibility* (New York: Norton, 1964), p. 222.
5. Robert Browning, "Rabbi Ben Ezra," *Poems of Robert Browning* (Boston: Houghton Mifflin, 1956), p. 281.

Chapter 6

1. Muriel James and Louis Savary, *A New Self: Self-Therapy with Transactional Analysis* (Reading, Mass.: Addison-Wesley, 1977), p. 251. See also Alfred Adler, *The Science of Living* (Garden City, New York: Anchor Books, 1969), pp. 113–130.

2. Emily Dickinson, "Parting," *A Little Treasury of Modern Poetry,* ed. Oscar Williams (New York: Scribner's, 1952), p. 44.
3. Lenor Madruga, *One Step at a Time* (New York: McGraw-Hill, 1979).
4. George Bach and Peter Wyden, *The Intimate Enemy: How to Fight Fair in Love and Marriage* (New York: Morrow, 1968).
5. Bach and Wyden, *The Intimate Enemy,* p. 343.
6. For more information on the stages summarized here, see Granger E. Westberg, *Good Grief: A Constructive Approach to the Problem of Loss.* (Philadelphia: Fortress Press, 1962). Used with permission of Fortress Press. A large-type edition of *Good Grief* is now available.
7. Li Po, "We Shall Grow Old Together," in *Chinese Love Poems: From Ancient to Modern Times* (New York: The Peter Pauper Press, 1954), p. 11.

Chapter 7

1. Honest intellectual intimacy has integrity; it is not a game plan or a tactic of manipulation. R. Buckminster Fuller, in *Earth, Inc.* (New York: Anchor Press/ Doubleday, 1973, p. 63), makes a plea for this kind of cooperative spirit between an individual and society:

> *The great aesthetic which will inaugurate the twenty-first century will be the utterly invisible quality of intellectual integrity; the integrity of the individual in dealing with his scientific discoveries; the integrity of the individual in dealing with conceptual realization of the comprehensive interrelatedness of all events; the integrity of the individual in dealing with the only experimentally arrived at information regarding invisible phenomena; and finally the integrity of all those who formulate invisibly within their respective minds and invisibly with the only mathematically dimensionable, advanced production technologies, on behalf of their fellow men.*

   Just as the individual's response to the universe must be marked with integrity, marriage partners must offer each other respect and honesty in their intellectual intimacy.
2. Dag Hammerskjold, *Markings,* trans. W. H. Auden and Leif Sjöberg (New York: Knopf, 1964), p. 105.
3. Plutarch, *Dialogue on Love,* in Julia O'Faolain and Laura Martines, eds., *Not in God's Image* (New York: Harper & Row, 1973), pp. 31–32.
4. I enjoy humor along with information and therefore often recommend Inge and Sten Hegeler, *An A B Z of Love,* trans. David Hohhen (New York: Alexicon Corp., 1967). Masters and Johnson's *The Pleasure Bond* (Boston: Little, Brown, 1975), and Alexander Lowen's *Love And Orgasm* (New York: Collier, Macmillan, 1965) are found useful by many couples.
5. Ashley Montague, "The Skin and Human Development," *Somantics,* Autumn 1977, p. 4.

6. H. Harlow, *Proceedings, American Philosophical Society,* no. 102, pp. 501–509, (1958).

7. R. B. Barnes, "Thermography of the Human Body," *Science,* 140: 870–877 (May 24, 1963).

8. Eric Berne, *Sex in Human Loving* (New York: Simon & Schuster, 1970), p. 126. See also Louis H. Forman and Janelle Smith Ramsburg, *Hello Sigmund, This Is Eric: Psychoanalysis and TA in Dialogue* (Mission, Kan.: Shedd Andrews and McMeel, Inc., 1978).

9. Eric Berne, *Intuition and Ego States* (San Francisco: TA Press, 1977), p. 4.

10. For more on projection, see James and Jongeward, *Born to Win* (Reading, Mass.: Addison-Wesley, 1971), pp. 244–245, 258–259.

11. Muriel James, "The Cure of Impotence with Transactional Analysis," in *Techniques in Transactional Analysis for Psychotherapists and Counselors* (Reading, Mass.: Addison-Wesley, 1977), p. 485.

12. Muriel James, *Transactional Analysis for Moms and Dads* (Reading, Mass.: Addison-Wesley, 1974), p. 10.

13. A not new, but still important, basic text is Gordon Allport, *The Nature of Prejudice* (Reading, Mass.: Addison-Wesley, 1954).

14. Frank Goble, *The Third Force: The Psychology of Abraham Maslow* (New York: Crossman, 1970), p. 32.

Chapter 8

1. George Bach and Peter Wyden, "Sex Rating Scale," from *The Intimate Enemy: How to Fight Fair in Love and Marriage* (New York: William Morrow & Co., copyright © 1968, 1969), pp. 260–261.

2. To learn more about target stroking on the job or in the home, see Muriel James, *The OK Boss* (Reading, Mass.: Addison-Wesley, 1975) and *Transactional Analysis for Moms and Dads* (Reading, Mass.: Addison-Wesley, 1975).

3. Muriel James and Louis Savary, *A New Self: Self-Therapy with Transactional Analysis* (Reading, Mass.: Addison-Wesley, 1977), p. 229.

4. John James, "The Game Plan," *Transactional Analysis Journal,* October 1976, pp. 14–17.

5. See Muriel James and Dorothy Jongeward, *The People Book* (Reading, Mass.: Addison-Wesley, 1975), pp. 177–180, for applications to adolescents, school, and family life.

Part Three

1. Hugh Prather, *Notes to Myself* (Moab, Utah: Real People Press, 1970), p. 1.

Chapter 9

1. Frederick Perls, *Gestalt Therapy Verbatim* (Moab, Utah: Real People Press, 1969), p. 4. All rights reserved.

2. For a look at Perls' script, see my chapter on him in Muriel James and Contributors, *Techniques in Transactional Analysis for Psychotherapists and Counselors* (Reading, Mass.: Addison-Wesley, 1977).
3. This discussion of the mathematics of relationships is based on Muriel James and Louis Savary, *A New Self: Self-Therapy with Transactional Analysis* (Reading, Mass.: Addison-Wesley, 1977), pp. 307–308. For a more complete explanation, see Muriel James and Louis Savary, *The Heart of Friendship* (New York: Harper & Row, 1976), especially Chapter 2, "The Third Self of Friendship," pp. 14–32.
4. Nikos Kazantzakis, *Report to Greco* (New York: Bantam Books, 1966).
5. Martin Buber, *Between Man and Man* (New York: Beacon Press, 1955), p. 92.
6. Frankl's theory, which he developed during his imprisonment in German concentration camps, asserts that people have the power to resist the forces of environment and an instinct to endure or rise above any situation. Here is one example of his own search for meaning in an intolerable situation:

   > *When the Nazis took this manuscript from him, he faced the prospect that neither he nor his work would survive. He escaped despair to which so many of his fellow inmates succumbed by asking himself: does the meaning of my life really depend on whether this manuscript gets published? He turned to other possible meanings, most of them immediate. The first was to survive, if possible, for the sake of his parents, wife, brother, and sister; more immediately still, his purpose was to help his fellow inmates in their despair. Although he was required to do hard labor up to eighteen hours a day, and was at one point reduced in weight to eighty pounds, he continued to practice his profession, organized secret discussion groups on mental hygiene, prompted other inmates to think about past achievements as well as tasks still waiting to be fulfilled.*

   Joseph Fabry, *The Pursuit of Meaning* (Boston: Beacon Press, 1969), p. 13. You may also want to read two books by Frankl himself: Viktor Frankl, *Man's Search for Meaning: An Introduction to Logotherapy* (Boston: Beacon Press, 1962), and *The Doctor and The Soul: From Psychotherapy to Logotherapy* (New York: Alfred Knopf, 1965).
7. For one-liner posters of hope to hang on your wall and enjoy, see Muriel James and John James, *Touch a Rainbow* (Millbrae, Calif.: Celestial Arts, 1978).
8. James and Contributors, *Techniques in Transactional Analysis,* p. 498.

Chapter 10

1. Dag Hammarskjold, *Markings* (London: Faber and Faber, 1964), p. 140.
2. Thanks to Mary and Robert Goulding for this idea.
3. Muriel James, *Transactional Analysis for Moms and Dads* (Reading, Mass.: Addison-Wesley, 1974), pp. 63–64.
4. "Social Readjustment Rating Scale," used by permission of Thomas H. Holmes, M.D., Professor of Psychiatry and Behavioral Sciences, University of Washington, Seattle, Washington.

5. Muriel James, *The OK Boss* (Reading, Mass.: Addison-Wesley, 1975), pp. 148–149.
6. For details see Muriel James, *Born to Love: Transactional Analysis in the Church* (Reading, Mass.: Addison-Wesley, 1973).

Epilogue

1. Pierre Teilhard de Chardin, *Activation of Energy* (New York: Harcourt Brace, 1971), p. 371.

PHOTO CREDITS

2 Frank Siteman, Stock, Boston, Inc. **8** Frank Siteman, Stock, Boston, Inc. **10** Jean-Claude LeJeane, Stock, Boston, Inc. **14** Courtesy Museum of Fine Arts, Boston **19** Photo by John Pearson, (c) 1979 **23** David Powers Photography **26** Marc Riboud, Magnum Photos **30** Karen Preuss, Jeroboam, Inc. **34** Martin Adler Levick, Black Star **37** Photography by Nina Leen, reproduced from *Images of Sound* by Nina Leen with permission of the author. Copyright (c) 1977 by Nina Leen, W. W. Norton & Co., Inc., New York **39** Tourism & Information Branch Photo, Government of the Yukon Territory **41** Photo by John Webb. Used by permission of Sherry and Dave Wilmer **44** Lisa Strawbridge **52** Top - IPA, Jeroboam, Inc. **52** Center - Suzanne Arms, Jeroboam, Inc. **52** Bottom - David Powers, Jeroboam, Inc. **53** Top - Hank Lebo, Jeroboam, Inc. **53** Center - Rick Smolan, Stock, Boston, Inc. **53** Bottom - Photography by Phil Preston, with permission of *The Boston Globe*. **66** Emilio Mercado, Jeroboam, Inc. **72** Karen Preuss, Jeroboam, Inc. **80** Photograph by Ulrike Welsch from *The World I Love to See,* with permission of *The Boston Globe.* **88** Photo by John Pearson, (c) 1979 **94** Richard Kalvar, Magnum Photos **97** Ron Benvenisti, Magnum Photos **102** Jeff Blechman **114** Lenor Madruga **119** Vince Compagnone, Jeroboam, Inc. **127** Richard Kalvar, Magnum Photos **132** Emilio Mercado, Jeroboam, Inc. **137** Top - Bob Clay, Jeroboam, Inc. **137** Center - Richard Lawrence Stack, Black Star **137** Bottom - Owen Franken, Stock, Boston, Inc. **140** Photo by John Pearson, (c) 1979 **149** Frank Siteman, Stock, Boston, Inc. **156** Emilio Mercado, Jeroboam, Inc. **162** Top - Owen Franken, Stock, Boston, Inc. **162** Center - Gabor Demjen, Stock, Boston, Inc. **162** Bottom - James R. Holland, Stock, Boston, Inc. **168** Emilio Mercado, Jeroboam, Inc. **182** Rose Skytta, Jeroboam, Inc. **188** Jeff Blechman **192** David Powers, Jeroboam, Inc. **195** Photo by John Pearson, (c) 1979 **202** Photo by Ulrike Welsch from *The World I Love to See,* with permission of *The Boston Globe.* **207** Photo by Ulrike Welsch from *The World I Love to See,* with permission of *The Boston Globe.* **214** Jeff Blankfort, Jeroboam, Inc. **230** Marshall Henrichs

Marriage is for Loving

Index